Prefaces to
Renaissance Literature

Prefaces to

Renaissance Literature

By DOUGLAS BUSH

CAMBRIDGE · MASSACHUSETTS

HARVARD UNIVERSITY PRESS

1966

Contents

Acknowledgments

THE GROUPING of these lectures was suggested by Mr. John Benedict of W. W. Norton & Company, Inc., who has brought the quintuplets to birth as a book. I am grateful to him and to Mr. George P. Brockway, president of the company, and to Dr. Thomas J. Wilson, director of the Harvard University Press, who have arranged joint publication in paperback and hard-cover form, respectively. I am indebted also to the several original sponsors or publishers of the lectures who have permitted reprinting: the Martin Foundation of Oberlin College, for the two lectures on "Classical Influences in Renaissance Literature," published by the Harvard University Press in 1952; the Claremont Graduate School and the Francis Bacon Foundation for the two lectures on "God and Nature" and "Time and Man" (1957); and the Columbia University Press for "The Isolation of the Renaissance Hero," published in *Reason and the Imagination: Studies in the His-*

tory of Ideas 1600–1800, edited by J. A. Mazzeo (1962). These names revive my pleasant memories of the cordial hospitality of Oberlin College, the Claremont Graduate School and its associated Colleges, and the University of Rochester.

Apart from a few verbal changes and some cutting and splicing and rewriting of introductory paragraphs to make the Foreword, the texts of the lectures remain as they were. Some things may be said more than once, but it seems better to leave repetitions than awkward lacunae. And no apology is needed for the repeating of some great quotations.

The bibliography includes a few items cited in the lectures and suggests books for further reading. The list had to be both limited and arbitrary, since the range of relevant topics, books, and articles is limitless; but many of the books named contain bibliographies.

D.B.

Foreword

As THE TITLE of this book suggests, these discussions are not contributions to the advancement of knowledge. They are reminders of the beliefs, ideas, and attitudes embodied in a mass of great literature that can never go out of date, however remote its world is from ours. In regard to most of the essentials of life, it is indeed not really remote, because we are still human beings, not completely mechanized but possessing some power to think and feel and choose and act in the face of good and evil, beauty and ugliness. Since the sixteenth and the earlier seventeenth centuries have long been recognized as one of the greatest ages of European and English literature, there would seem to be sufficient excuse for dwelling now and then on some of the central and obvious aspects and causes of that greatness, on the literary, ethical, and religious principles that combined, in a world of abundant corruption and violence, to provide a creed and an outlook founded in

ix

realistic sanity and strength and imaginative vision. The result was a body of literature that embraces birdlike songs and heroic poems, earth-shaking comedy and earth-shaking tragedy. We return to that body of literature because it is infinitely enjoyable, but the experience may help us as individuals to regain some elements of health and taste and imagination that are not conspicuous in our own time. Nowadays we are, it seems, both terribly complex personalities and helpless nodes in a communication network; but the simplicities of Shakespeare and others are still there, and it is possible that he and his fellows would have thought us somewhat deranged or immature.

Before we come to our general topics, which are spacious enough, we might put them into some focus by taking brief account of changing views of the Renaissance as a whole. Everyone has met the classic definitions summed up in various phrases: man's discovery of himself, of his inner and outer world; the assertion of individualism against the authoritarian uniformity and anonymity of the Middle Ages; the secularization of the human mind and human life; and so on.

These and kindred definitions, which came from such famous historians as Michelet and Burckhardt, were for a time settled axioms, and they still have popular currency; moreover, they have truth in them. But, from our present point —or rather, our diverse points—of view, they are much oversimplified and lopsided. Just now I will make only three general comments. First, these classic definitions are mainly based on the Italian Renaissance, and even in regard to that they need much modification; they are still more misleading when applied, as they often have been, to the Renaissance in northern Europe and England. Secondly, the historians who launched these definitions were immersed in the current of nineteenth-century liberalism and were disposed to see the Renaissance as the great secular emancipation. Thirdly, this strong bias was coupled with what was as yet a quite inadequate knowledge and comprehension of the Middle Ages, so that the Renaissance appeared as a triumphant awakening from a thousand-year sleep.

To see how far the pendulum can swing, we may observe that some modern religious thinkers, like Reinhold Niebuhr, and some modern critics and poets have seen the Renaissance, not as a glorious dawn after a long dark night, but as the great upsurge of secular pride that has brought the world to its present unhappy state. Most historical scholars, who are in the tradition of secular liberalism, would not accept such a view, but the fact that it can be held at all indicates at least that the study of the Renaissance does not mean merely surveying a set pattern in which everything has its unquestioned place and value. As a special example, while Shakespeare has commonly been considered, in regard to religion, a sceptic or an indifferent bystander, many critics of recent years have insisted that his serious plays embody a positively Christian strain, and of course this view has met opposition or strong qualification.

While there is no need to labor the obvious, we might consider how we would go about summing up the civilization of our own age and country if we wanted to leave a capsule outline for the benefit of historians—or lecturers—four centuries hence. Some things, like the convulsions and anxieties of hot and cold wars and the spectacular advances of science and technology, would be relatively easy. But what of the spiritual and ethical temper and the literary and artistic products of our culture? With respect to religion, would we stress the statistics of church membership, or the unthinking materialism of masses of people, or the fundamentalism of "the Bible belt," or the religious thought of men like Niebuhr and Paul Tillich? With respect to literature, or at least reading, would we base our judgment on mass media and bestsellers or on Frost, Eliot, Stevens, Hemingway, Faulkner, and others? Would we say that the literature and thought of the past are a dynamic element in the lives of a great many or of a very few? And then suppose that we enlarge our horizon from the modern American scene to take in other countries and several centuries? In short, although earlier cultures seem to have had much more homogeneity than ours, we cannot speak of such abstractions as "the medieval mind" or "the Renaissance mind." The truth about a rich age is very complex, and every observer has his limitations of knowledge and understanding, his Idols of the Cave.

All this has been a comment on traditional views of the Renaissance, but it has a bearing on the present small enterprise. As I have already indicated, the purpose of these discourses is not to plough up new ground, still less to dig a hole, but only to recall some central features of a familiar landscape, a landscape we are perhaps content to leave to college courses, even though it is so permanently attractive and stirring. Some reasons for the greatness of Renaissance literature, such as the birth of men of genius, may be taken as acts of God. Some other things, from the invention of printing to the accumulation of capital, are large facts in the background. But some things that are at the center of our subject can be looked into, or looked at. In all of these discussions we are more or less concerned with the interaction of the two great traditions of western culture, the classical and the Christian. Neither of those traditions seems to be notably active in most writing of our time, and some of our chief clichés have to do with a general consciousness of hollowness and confusion; one minor symptom is the erratic quest of young critics for "Christ figures" in modern literature. It is of course a question how far we can live in or on the past, but we can assuredly find there qualities of vision and utterance that are apparently no longer attainable. We may covet what we cannot share.

Prefaces to

Renaissance Literature

I

Humanism and the Critical Spirit

CLASSICAL INFLUENCE on the literature of the Renaissance is a huge subject. It requires a minute survey of antiquity, the Middle Ages, and the Renaissance, the whole web of life, thought, and literature in half a dozen countries during many centuries. One could try to cover the vast territory with the factual and even-handed justice of an encyclopedia article, but the result would be painfully arid. On the other hand, to stick to two or three major topics, such as the complex and all-embracing influence of Plato and Cicero, would be to offer a sketch of the sun and moon as a picture of the universe. For instance, if we were to discuss the influence of Plato, we should need more than two hours to consider Plato's own thought, Neoplatonism, the assimilation of Platonic elements into early Christianity, the development of the tradition in the Middle Ages, the continuance of Neoplatonism in the Renaissance along with renewed study of Plato himself, the work of such earnest Christian Platonists as Marsilio Ficino, the great translator and expositor; and then the various kinds of Platonic and Neoplatonic influence ranging from the work of Erasmus, More, and Sir Thomas Elyot to the religion of beauty in women or the scientific thought of Copernicus and Galileo. So it seems best not to put all our eggs in one basket, even a Platonic one, but to scramble them.

It is hardly necessary to say that, while one has to generalize freely, all generalities are subject to many exceptions and qualifications. Among many things that must be omitted, apart from occasional reference, is the great mass of writing in Latin, both utilitarian and imaginative; the names of Ficino, Erasmus, and More are sufficient reminders that literature in the international language was of the first importance, but a large part of it has sunk below the horizon. Finally, some things will have to be taken for granted, such as the different and the changing social, economic, political, and religious conditions in the various countries, the effects of geographical discovery, and other factors outside of literature proper. Some modern historians, by the way, seem inclined to explain the Renaissance in terms of these causes and to minimize classical influence, but it is difficult for anyone concerned with literature and thought to follow them.

The classical revival of the fifteenth and sixteenth centuries was a great example of the logical and inevitable recurrence of an historical pattern. In ancient times, when Greek civilization had run its course, Greece was conquered by the virile and relatively uncivilized Romans. The Romans absorbed, in their own way, the culture of Greece and, under the expanding dominion of Rome, Greco-Roman culture spread over most of Europe, to be in time penetrated, not without conflicts, by Christianity. Then the empire in its decay was overrun by the virile and uncivilized barbarians, and once again the conquerors had to be educated by the conquered, now in a more or less Christian world. That long process of re-education was the Renaissance. At first there were, from Italy to Ireland, only a few oases of Greco-Roman-Christian culture, which flourished because of undisturbed continuity or quick revival. One conspicuous early phase was the Carolingian Renaissance. By the twelfth and thirteenth centuries the movement had gained much greater breadth and momentum; it embraced science, philosophy, literature, and art. Thus the rich and many-sided Renaissance of the fifteenth and sixteenth centuries, which we think of as *the* Renaissance, was only the brilliant climax of the process of a thousand years. And indeed we should not say "climax," since two important impulses of the Renaissance, sceptical rationalism and experimental science, developed mainly in later centuries and cannot be said to have generally dominated thought and life until the twentieth.

All this, to be sure, is commonplace, but in looking at literature we need to keep the large perspective in mind. If we do, we shall not, like some of the early humanists and some nineteenth-century historians, fall into the delusion of seeing the Renaissance as a sudden phenomenon—although the contagion of enthusiasm, the invention of printing, and other causes made the later stages relatively rapid. We shall not, moreover, in thinking of the classical revival in the various European countries, assume that all the cultural clocks are running on the same schedule. And we shall not be surprised by the stubborn vitality, throughout the Renaissance, of medieval books, attitudes, and ideas, or by what often seems to be an incongruous mixture in individual minds; we have the same kind of mixtures in our own age and in ourselves. Perhaps it should be added that the word "medieval," which I just used, was not a synonym for "bad" or "muddle-headed."

If the classical revival produced rich fruit and not mere wax flowers, one main reason was the strength of medieval and Christian traditions and beliefs.

In the history of the various countries—and in that of individual writers—the classical Renaissance had three natural stages: discovery, assimilation, and re-expression. The story of the discovery or rediscovery, in the fourteenth and fifteenth centuries, of Latin and Greek manuscripts has been told at large by such scholars as Voigt, Symonds, Sandys, and Sabbadini, and it is an often dramatic and exciting story, but it can be only touched upon here. The early humanists who hunted so eagerly for manuscripts, and who brought to light so many neglected and forgotten works of ancient literature, were likely to heap contempt upon the churchmen and scholastics who had allowed them to gather dust in cathedral and monastic libraries. Such contempt was doubtless pardonable. But we should remember some other facts as well: that many of the chief works of Latin literature, as wholes or in parts, and Latin translations of some Greek writings, had been studied throughout the Middle Ages; that a knowledge of Greek had flourished or at least existed at some periods in some places in various countries of the West; that it was largely through the labors of generations of monks that the manuscripts were there to be found; and, finally, we might wonder if a humanist who visited the classical sections of our public and college libraries might not find some dust.

Under the heading of discovery and propagation, we may remind ourselves again of the importance of printing. Although much early, and much later, printing could hardly bear comparison with manuscripts, the rapid multiplication of texts by the printing press obviously and immensely hastened the circulation of all kinds of knowledge. A special place in the history of the classical revival has always been given to Aldus Manutius of Venice, the great scholar-printer who issued so many noble editions of Greek and Latin authors. Later in the sixteenth century there was the French family of scholar-printers, the Estiennes, who themselves wrote important books, dictionaries and other things.

Along with printers must be remembered the countless scholars, from Erasmus and Budé and Vives down to the more or less obscure, who edited the classical authors, who did all the inglorious but essential journey-work of scholarship, who wrote the books that recreated the ancient world as an historical scene, and who adapted the principles and practice of ancient education to the use of modern and Christian peoples. A number of these scholars, among them some whose elegant Latin won them posts in the papal service, had literary zeal unhampered by morals or manners, such as Poggio Bracciolini, hunter of manuscripts, moral essayist, and compiler of a book of off-color anecdotes, whose conscience, late in life, impelled him to marry and, as a prelude, to cast off his mistress, the mother of his fourteen children. Some highly respectable men were pure scholars, devoted to philological and historical learning, such as Budé (who was said to have made the sacrifice of working only three hours on his wedding day), although even he wrote a treatise on education. Still others, like Erasmus and Vives and Melanchthon, were Christian humanists in a full, broad, and active sense. For them classical learning was a means rather than an end. They looked back "to the fountains," pagan and Christian, to find a working ideal for the civilization of the present and future. We shall be coming back to that ideal; indeed we can seldom get far away from it.

Literature includes the literature of knowledge as well as of power, and we must take some account of that heterogeneous mass of writing if we are to appreciate the full effects of

5

the classical revival. There could be no advance in knowledge until men had first caught up with the achievements of antiquity. In the realm of mere knowledge, accordingly, the scholars and teachers who were editing, translating, and propagating the classics were the party of progress; they were leading mankind back to the main road of civilization, from which it had wandered into what they looked upon as the arid desert of scholasticism. Since we cannot survey all the branches of knowledge, we will take two diverse examples, the development of science and the development of historical writing.

We do not now think of the Middle Ages as a long blank period in the history of science. Some names and facts have of course been familiar for centuries, and recent historians have revealed a far greater range of genuine scientific activity than earlier writers suspected. Yet it remains true that most of the great and less great minds were preoccupied with other things than science and that what we should call a scientific attitude was uncommon. For a representative treasury of early medieval misinformation, there is Bishop Isidore of Seville's encyclopedia, the *Etymologies*. One random item, which is undoubtedly true, will not be found in the *Britannica:* "If an eel is killed in wine, people who drink of it have an aversion for wine." But we might quote more central observations on astronomy and physiology:

> The sun, which is made of fire, develops a whiter heat because of the extreme speed of its circular motion. Its fire, philosophers say, is fed with water, and receives the virtue of light and heat from a contrary element. Hence we see that it is often wet and dewy.

> The spleen has its name from being a *supplement* to the liver, on the opposite side, so that there might be no

6

vacuum, and this some men think was formed on account of laughter. For it is by the spleen that we laugh, by the bile we are angry, by the heart we are wise, by the liver we love. While these four elements remain, the creature is whole.[1]

Nine centuries later, in the notable year 1543, came the revolutionary works of Copernicus on the astronomical system and Vesalius on the human body. From this time onward the story of science may be called a story of continuous and sometimes spectacular progress—though we may remember that the works of Isidore and his kind were printed and reprinted throughout the Renaissance "enlightenment," and that a geocentric world, astrological medicine, and similar doctrines held their ground until well on in the seventeenth century. If we ask what Copernicus and Vesalius have to do with the classics, the answer is that influence was both direct and indirect. Copernicus, in seeking an explanation of phenomena more economical than Ptolemy's, owed something to ancient theories of the earth's movements and to mathematical Neoplatonists of the Renaissance. In biology and medicine there were the treatises of Aristotle and Theophrastus, of Hippocrates' followers and Galen, which helped to establish an attitude and a method; these works, whatever their errors, were records of the interrogation of nature, not uncritical repetitions of traditional and half-occult lore.

As for the indirect influence of the classics, we may approach it by way of Bacon's censure of scholastic logic and the pseudo-sciences as two of the three principal diseases that had hindered the advancement of learning. Scholastic phi-

1. For the three quotations from Isidore of Seville, see his *Etymologiarum . . . Libri XX*, ed. W. M. Lindsay (Oxford Classical Texts), XII.vi.25, III.xlix, XI.i.127; and Ernest Brehaut, "An Encyclopedist of the Dark Ages: Isidore of Seville," *Studies in History, Economics and Public Law*, XLVIII (New York: Columbia University Press, 1912).

losophy, originally a great demonstration of faith in human reason and the right of inquiry into the nature of man's world, had come to be the antithesis of the scientific attitude, and Bacon was disposed to condemn both root and branch. The scholastic fallacy, as Bacon saw it, was an unfruitful devotion to logic and metaphysics, to unknowable final causes, along with indifference to observed fact and to the consequent extension of man's power over nature. Although Bacon's scientific aims were different from, in some ways antagonistic to, those of most classical humanists, he and others inherited their hostility to degenerate scholasticism. The general impetus of humanism, the quest of real and useful truth freed from medieval accretions, had a very great influence in stimulating the spirit of critical inquiry and thus in creating an atmosphere favorable to the growth of science.

If as a rule the classical humanists, with such exceptions as Rabelais, took relatively small interest in science itself, and hence came in time to be regarded by the scientific as a party of reaction rather than of progress, one reason was that the humanists were concerned, not with man's control over nature, but with the much harder problem of man's control over himself. Further, the ethical idealism that the humanists imbibed from the ancient moralists and the Christian tradition was not altogether in harmony with the behavioristic view of man inaugurated by such diverse explorers of anatomy and motivation as Vesalius and Machiavelli; and Bacon, in his role of practical psychologist, gave thanks to Machiavelli and others "that write what men do, and not what they ought to do." But if Erasmus, for instance, continually upheld the Christian and classical ideal of what men ought to do, he also, more than any other individual, awakened the conscience of Europe to the folly and wickedness of what men did do; and Vives, who shared fully in Erasmus' religious, moral, and educational effort, was at the same time a realistic pioneer in psychology and sociology.

When we turn to our second example of classical influence in the field of knowledge, the understanding and the writing of history, we find a parallel process. Medieval world-histories and chronicles, apart from a few remarkable books like Bede's *Ecclesiastical History*, were likely to be tendentious works in the tradition—although not on the level—of Augustine's *City of God*, or uncritical compilations of fact and legend, or unphilosophical annals of contemporary events like the Anglo-Saxon Chronicle. Of the Greek and Roman world in particular, few medieval men approached an historical view. The "matter of Rome the great" included the myths and legends of Troy, Thebes, Alexander, Julius Caesar, and almost anything else not contained in the matters of France and of Britain. One notable example of romantic historiography is the legend of New Troy, which was firmly established by Geoffrey of Monmouth in the twelfth century and was not finally demolished until the early seventeenth. According to this legend, Britain, like other nations of western Europe, had an eponymous Trojan ancestor. Brutus or Brute, a great-grandson of Aeneas, having to flee westward, settled with his followers in Albion and became the progenitor of a long line of kings. The many related stories were rehearsed by generations of chroniclers and celebrated by Elizabethan poets and dramatists; Shakespeare's contribution was of course *King Lear* and *Cymbeline*. The chief early sceptic was the Italian humanist, Polydore Vergil, who worked at the court of Henry VII and Henry VIII and who applied to this mass of legend the critical lessons he had learned from ancient history. During the sixteenth century and later, Polydore was denounced by patriotic historians; he was a delirious foreigner who with one dash of a pen had cashiered threescore princes together. But moralists came to doubt the glory of descent from "Venus, that lascivious adulteress," and the whole structure of legend was undermined by such sophisticated students of history as William Camden and John Selden. Yet the poet Michael Drayton could utter a wistful sigh for the tales "Which now the envious world doth slander for a dream," and Milton could salute the nymph of the Severn as

> Virgin, daughter of Locrine,
> Sprung of old Anchises' line.

Henceforth, however, British history, sadly shortened, was to begin with the bald, unromantic figure of Julius Caesar.

There are many examples, in many areas, of the growth of the historical spirit. The medieval man was likely to see his cherished Latin authors rather as names attached to wise or entertaining books than as men who lived in particular places in particular times; and he might see Tullius and Cicero as two persons. The development of an historical consciousness —and of esthetic discrimination—was of course one of the great marks of the Renaissance mind, and it showed itself in Petrarch. Two generations after Petrarch we meet such an exemplar of mature and active classical scholarship as Laurentius or Lorenzo Valla, who not only put the study of Latin style and idiom on a new basis but turned his acutely critical learning upon momentous documents: he proved that the Donation of Constantine, which had long buttressed papal claims to temporal power, was a forgery, and he assigned to a date much later than the apostolic age that rich source of medieval and Renaissance Neoplatonism that went under the name of Dionysius the Areopagite. Valla also made the first scholarly criticism of errors in the Latin Vulgate, in notes which Erasmus later published. Erasmus, the greatest of all popularizers of classical *humanitas* and "the philosophy of Christ," paid tribute to Valla and urged the necessity of applying scholarship to sacred as well as other texts. His edition in 1516 of the Greek New Testament was an act of courage no less than of religious and scholarly zeal, since for over a thousand years the Latin Vulgate had been in official use as virtually the word of God himself. And one might add here the name of John Colet, the friend of Erasmus and More, Dean of St. Paul's and founder of St. Paul's School. Colet was no classical humanist, but he had studied in Italy and had some new light; and while the professor of divinity at Oxford lectured on Duns Scotus, Colet lectured there on St. Paul's epistles. Although his main purpose was naturally interpretation and application, he treated the epistles, not as parts of an anonymous and timeless (and allegorical) Bible, but as letters written by a certain man in a certain historical milieu.

As for the theory and practice of historical writing, it was the ancients who taught that. By the sixteenth century the Roman historians, and the Greek historians in Latin versions, were available, and, as the century went on, both Romans and Greeks were put into the modern languages (sometimes by circuitous routes, as in Thomas Nicolls' English translation of a French translation of Valla's Latin translation of Thucydides). As a result, historiography entered upon a new era. Chronicles and world-histories on the medieval pattern continued to be written and read, but these gradually gave way to more sophisticated histories whose authors had profited from the ancients. The methods, if not the genius, of the classical historians, which a very few medieval writers had approached, became in time more general—the rejection of the fabulous and improbable, the use of documents, the weighing of evidence, the analysis of cause and effect, the effort toward coherent philosophical interpretation of characters and events. Early representatives of the new outlook and method were Machiavelli and Guicciardini. Machiavelli is perhaps not, either as man or as thinker, very attractive, but one much-quoted passage from a letter, written when he had been dismissed from his official post and was occupied on his small estate, shows the classical humanist in a gracious light:

> At nightfall I return home and seek my writing room, and, divesting myself on its threshold of my rustic garments, stained with mud and mire, I assume courtly attire, and thus suitably clothed, enter within the ancient courts of ancient men, by whom, being cordially welcomed, I am fed with the food that alone is mine, and for which I was born, and am not ashamed to hold discourse with them, and inquire the motives of their actions; and these men in their humanity reply to me, and for the space of four hours I feel no weariness, remember no trouble, no longer fear poverty, no longer dread death; my whole being is absorbed in them.

Although in his chief work Machiavelli drew political lessons for his own time from the pages of Livy, he had much less affinity with that mellow *laudator temporis acti* than with the shrewdly analytical and cynical Tacitus. In the sixteenth and seventeenth centuries Tacitus was esteemed the very bible of statesmen and, in addition to being a model, for anti-Ciceronians, of concise and epigrammatic style, he had a large share in creating a mundane and realistic view of history. Bacon's *Henry VII* was one product of that school. On the other hand, there was a less readily definable but more idealistic theory of history which had distinctively medieval as well as classical roots. For many writers and readers of the Renaissance, as in earlier times, history was not the analysis of power politics, in the world or within the state, but ethical philosophy teaching by examples, a panorama of God's judgments upon rulers and empires. It was largely in that spirit, although not without elements of "realism," that Sir Walter Ralegh wrote his *History of the World,* and his religious vision inspired some noble and impassioned meditations on the greatness and the littleness of man. We might try to imagine, on the page of a modern social scientist, a parallel to this half-medieval, half-classical prose poem on life and death,

> towards which we always travel both sleeping and waking: neither have those beloved companions of honor and riches any power at all, to hold us any one day, by the promises of glorious entertainments; but by what crooked path soever we walk, the same leadeth on directly to the house of death, whose doors lie open at all hours, and to all persons. For this tide of man's life, after it once turneth and declineth, ever runneth with a perpetual ebb and falling stream, but never floweth again: our leaf once fallen, springeth no more, neither doth the sun or the summer adorn us again, with the garments of new leaves and flowers.[2]

If we, like Matthew Arnold, are disturbed by Ralegh's speculations about the site of paradise and other problems which would have been impossible for the critical mind of Thucydides, we might remember, for instance, that Jerome Cardan, the eminent Italian scientist of the previous generation, held that a city's political power would be great if the tail of the Great Bear were vertical over it (a view attacked by the still more eminent Jean Bodin, who had his own occult in-

2. Sir Walter Ralegh, *History of the World,* I.ii.5 (ed. 1614), p. 31; *Works* (Oxford University Press, 1829), II, 60–61. Matthew Arnold's comments are in his "On the Modern Element in Literature," *Matthew Arnold: On the Classical Tradition,* ed. R. H. Super (Ann Arbor: University of Michigan Press, 1960).

stincts).[3] And it might be added that something akin to the spirit of Ralegh's book has informed a massive work of our age, Toynbee's *Study of History*—to the distress of "pure" historians and rationalistic liberals.

If we had time, we could follow up a similar double strain in the art of biography. For writers and readers who favored the realistic kind of history, there was such a biographical model as Suetonius' lives of the Roman emperors, which were put into English by the great translator of the early seventeenth century, Philemon Holland. For the more orthodox believer in ethical examples, there was Plutarch, who for centuries held a high place in the reading of old and young. Plutarch had the good fortune to be turned into felicitous French by Amyot and from French into the still more felicitous English of Sir Thomas North. The power of North's translation is not merely a matter of word and rhythm; it arises from a feeling that he shared with other men of the age, a reverence for the special greatness of ancient heroes combined with an instinctive sense of contemporaneous intimacy. Hence he ranges freely from the colloquial and slangy to the poetic, and on all levels he is dramatic. As everyone knows, North received the finest of tributes in having some passages, such as the description of Cleopatra's barge, taken over by Shakespeare with little more change than was needed to put them into verse.

We have looked, briefly, at two fields of knowledge and have seen something of the ancient critical spirit in operation. We took science as one example because it might be too readily assumed that that kind of knowledge developed altogether independently. But it was the humanities, history

3. On Cardan and Bodin, see *Method for the Easy Comprehension of History By John Bodin, Translated by Beatrice Reynolds* (New York: Columbia University Press, 1945), pp. xix, 232–33.

(which was not yet a social science), philosophy, and literature that were most deeply rooted in ancient wisdom. These liberal studies, *litterae humaniores*, were concerned with man as man, as a rational and ethical being and not as a professional or technical specialist. While the universities largely maintained their scholastic and professional curricula (although these were modified by humanism), education in the schools of Europe was pretty thoroughly classical. Teachers of the Renaissance period were far more numerous and better equipped than their medieval predecessors, and they had the whole extant body of classical literature to use; but the basic aim of Renaissance education might still have been summed up in the words of the twelfth-century John of Salisbury, "the knowledge of virtue that makes a good man." We may recall the similar utterances of Erasmus and Vives and Roger Ascham and Milton and many other men. Everywhere in the dozens of Renaissance treatises on education we find the twin ideal, virtue and good letters. It might of course be said that the enunciation of such ideals only corresponded to our Commencement addresses; that, since thousands of teachers cannot all be geniuses, there was much uninspired gerund-grinding; and that in many schoolrooms the only active Muse was "Lady Birch." Still, when we have made allowance for such human frailties and for practical, professional motives behind the study of Latin, there remains ample evidence that in all the literary countries there was an extraordinary number of notable teachers, many of them writers too, and that— as Rabelais' Gargantua and many other witnesses attest— there was an extraordinary enthusiasm for good letters, very often for virtue as well.

I should like to mention one example, an admittedly special example, of the realization in actual life of classical-Christian ideals. Perhaps the greatest Italian teacher of the earlier fifteenth century was Vittorino da Feltre. He labored with such zeal, piety, and gaiety in his all-embracing role as teacher of Latin and Greek, spiritual guide, athletic director, and nurse, that he was not, as we grimly say, a productive scholar; his life was given to his pupils. But one of those pupils happened to be the Federigo who became ruler of the little principality of Urbino. Under Federigo and his son, Urbino was renowned, even in Renaissance Italy, as a center of the finest culture, and it remains famous because it was mirrored in the finest of all courtesy books, *The Courtier* of Castiglione. Castiglione, a minor diplomat, was himself an ideal gentleman, versed in literature and painting, a poet and a friend of artists and writers, and no one could set forth with fuller authority the attributes of the ideal gentleman and amateur who, in addition to public service, makes life itself an art. Thus in a book partly based on Cicero's *De Oratore*—one of the half-dozen ancient treatises that created the formative ideals of Renaissance education—we have pictured an aristocratic group whose way of life was the flower of humanistic teaching. If the word "aristocratic" offends some ears, it may be said that Vittorino, who had been poor himself, took in as pupils poor boys who could not pay fees, that this kind of aristocratic education was being given to all and sundry in the thousands of European grammar schools (such as that in Stratford on Avon), and that education was conceived of in terms of the highest, not the lowest, common denominator.

During the Renaissance and well through the nineteenth century, all students all over Europe were brought up on the same body of literature, and study of that literature meant a unified literary, historical, political, ethical, and metaphysical knowledge and understanding. It is impossible to exaggerate the significance of the fact that all educated men, including scientists, held the classical heritage in common; that they had, or at any rate started from, a common experience and outlook, and were united by a uniform and universal bond of solidarity, stronger in some ways than such dividing forces as the Reformation and rising nationalism. I do not mean that all men thought alike; the classics could be invoked, as we shall partly see, to support political or ethical or religious orthodoxy and also democratic or sceptical or naturalistic rebellion. But there was a broad highway that all men traveled, and both those who stayed on it and those who departed from it knew where they were going.

The importance of such a universal tradition we should be qualified to appreciate, after many decades of a chaotic elective system and vastly expanded curriculum. In his *Three Centuries of Harvard*, Professor Morison says that "Mr. Eliot, more than any other man, is responsible for the greatest educational crime of the century against American youth—depriving him of his classical heritage." [4] Of late years our colleges have been trying to install some kind of backbone among the floating ribs, appendixes, and adipose tissue of education; and in the world at large much earnest study has been given to problems of communication among widely different cultural groups and nations. The same problem of heterogeneous diversity of knowledge and outlook is conspicuously illustrated in modern poetry. In contrast with the private symbolism of so much modern writing, a Renaissance poet anywhere in Europe could assume in his readers a common stock of knowledge and for the most part a common outlook, and he could draw freely upon the traditional and international gold reserve. If the gold sometimes turned into brass, the same thing may happen to the most original private symbols.

4. Samuel Eliot Morison, *Three Centuries of Harvard 1636–1936* (Cambridge: Harvard University Press, 1937), pp. 389–90.

A related fact or attitude, also traditional and international, was the conception of imaginative literature and its function. Sixty-five years ago Spingarn began his well-known book with the statement that "The first problem of Renaissance criticism was the justification of imaginative literature." [5] Throughout the Middle Ages, and the Renaissance as well, Plato's objections to poetry were recurrently fortified by Christian objections to pagan and often immoral writings. These Platonic and patristic and "puritan" complaints were met, during the Middle Ages and not seldom in the Renaissance, by the doctrine of allegorical truth contained beneath the husk of fiction. This allegorical and defensive method of exegesis, which had been practiced in Greece before Plato, was later applied to both the Bible and the classics, notably the *Aeneid* and even the more doubtful poetry of Ovid, and it was given a popular restatement for the Renaissance by Boccaccio. Aristotle's *Poetics*, which was rediscovered about 1500, in time raised this and other fundamental questions to a new level. Plato's ethical objection to poetry, that it stirred up harmful emotions, was countered by Aristotle's theory of catharsis (however that theory might be interpreted); and Plato's metaphysical objection was invalidated by Aristotle's doctrine of ideal imitation, that art was not two removes from truth, since it was a rendering, not of the particular, but of the universal and probable. Thus the Aristotelian esthetic established imaginative literature on a firm foundation. In England, as elsewhere, moralists could still complain, and the allegorical conception remained strong, but Sir Philip Sidney at least could take his stand on Aristotelian imitation —and could also marshal Platonic arguments on behalf of poetry against Platonic objections. However, poetry owed

5. Joel E. Spingarn, *A History of Literary Criticism in the Renaissance* (New York: Macmillan, 1899 and later editions), p. 3.

perhaps as much to the allegorical tradition as to Aristotle.

The gradual change brought about by the circulation of Aristotelian ideas did not apparently weaken the ethical view of poetry that prevailed in the Renaissance. Aristotle's own view of poetry was indeed essentially ethical. And when we think not merely of Plato and Aristotle but of Aristophanes and Horace and Plutarch and others, we may say that in antiquity the accepted function of literature was the making of good men and good citizens. To say that is not to say that writers were all or always didactic, or that the ethical conception meant preaching or in any way detracted from the qualities that belong to great writing; the place that the Greeks and Romans have held in world literature is sufficient reassurance on that point. The idea of delightful teaching was strongly reinforced in the Renaissance; through the imagination and emotions men might be stirred to the active love of public and private virtue. For serious humanists in the sixteenth century, as in the twelfth, even the ancient writers of licentious comedy and satire contained moral instruction, somewhat obliquely presented, and the philosophers—Plato, Cicero, and Seneca in particular—had, through the limited but authentic light of natural reason, come close to Christian ideals of righteousness. On the fusion of pagan wisdom with Christianity one could quote countless moving testimonies, from some of the Church Fathers onward to Petrarch and Erasmus and many English authors from Sir Thomas Elyot to Milton. Not all humanists and imaginative writers, to be sure, were conspicuous for virtue or religion, since the classical revival, especially in Italy and France, had its neopagans. But no one who has hearkened to the cloud of witnesses on the other side can doubt either the sincerity of their ethical creed or the strength that much of the greatest Renaissance writing derived from it.

II

The Classics and
Imaginative Literature

WE MIGHT as well admit, some time, that when we use the word "classical" in a broad sense, as a rule we don't have a very clear notion of what we mean. We may say, quite truly, that the word applies to such writers as Molière and Racine, Milton and Jane Austen, and that it does not apply to such writers as Blake and Shelley and Whitman and D. H. Lawrence. And perhaps that leaves us wiser. If we want more direct criteria and survey the Greek writers from Homer to Theocritus or Lucian, we have considerable trouble in naming qualities of outlook and style that are common to all alike. The effort may not get beyond some such answer as "Centrality, sanity, and concrete clarity of vision and expression, focused upon the actualities of human nature and life, and not refracted or blurred by the various kinds of religious or secular prepossessions and subjectivity that came with medieval and modern culture." And that, even if acceptable, is not very usable.

But the word "classical" covers the Romans as well as the Greeks, and if we check our definition in the light of Latin literature from Lucretius and Catullus to Tacitus and Martial, we must bring in so many positive or negative modifications that we are further still from a uniform and usable criterion. We may agree on the solid initial fact that Roman literature in general, compared with the Greek, was itself "neoclassical," since it embodied many of the formal and rhetorical elements which the modern period of so-called neoclassicism greatly prized and carried to frequent excess. Moreover, the Middle Ages, the Renaissance, and the neoclassical age were nourished preponderantly on Latin literature and usually regarded it as the standard. It is, by the way, one of the signal proofs of Dryden's critical discernment and candor that, at the height of the neoclassical age in England, he could contrast Chaucer's forthright naturalness of apprehension and expression with Ovid's incessant rhetorical tricks and see the medieval poet as a more truly classical writer than the ancient. Not, we may add, that Chaucer was a naïve or uneducated poet, or unaware of medieval and Ovidian rhetoric; but his mature vision was focused directly on the object and the idea. All this is only an elaborate warning that neoclassicism was often unclassical, and that the greatest writers of the Renaissance—including the greatest of English classicists, Milton—were, happily, not altogether classicized. If, in the ensuing discussion, an undue amount of evidence is taken from English literature, it is partly because the writer is not a universal doctor and partly because the limitation of space favors the use of what is most generally familiar.

Men of the Renaissance had a profound reverence for the ancient poets, philosophers, orators, statesmen and heroes as a superior race, and this was a dynamic faith, not a genteel tradition. As modern literature and science and civilization developed, progressives might deny any such inherent superiority and set up the moderns against the ancients, but that note of protest was seldom heard before 1600. The true spirit of veneration and imitation was expressed by such a bold intelligence as Valla, in the preface to his work on Latin style. In the place of the old Roman empire, he says, there remains the universal sway of the Roman language, in which are contained all the disciplines worthy of a free man: when the language flourishes, all branches of knowledge flourish, and when it dies, they die; for who have been the great thinkers, orators, jurists, authors, if not those men who have striven most studiously to speak well? More than a century after Valla, the same faith was stated with even simpler piety by Thomas Wilson in his *Arte of Rhetorique:*

> Now before we use either to write or speak eloquently, we must dedicate our minds wholly to follow the most wise and learned men, and seek to fashion as well their speech and gesturing as their wit or inditing. The which when we earnestly mind to do, we cannot but in time appear somewhat like them.

Such imitative zeal could of course lead to wrongheadedness. The sometimes extravagant worship and imitation of Cicero's style drew a famous satire from Erasmus and a famous censure from Bacon, who saw the study of words instead of matter as one of the main obstacles in the way of progress. On the other hand, Cicero was in fact not only the chief creator of modern prose style but the chief ethical teacher and civilizer of Europe; and Erasmus, while he satirized misguided and frivolous Ciceronianism, was himself a reverent admirer of the almost Christian moralist. It might be said further that Bacon was really attacking the whole tradition of humanistic education, with much the same prejudices as John Dewey's, and that the great humanists did not put words before matter. Their matter was the nature of man and society, and they were wisely conscious of the relations between style and the general pattern of ethical and social order. We may say of them what Mr. Trilling has said of that authentic later humanist, Matthew Arnold, that whenever he talks about style he is talking about society.[1] If we are sceptical about such a relationship, there is an obvious answer in the parallel between the state of the modern world and the modern soul and the more disordered manifestations of literary and pictorial art.

Sir Philip Sidney, the first important English classicist, supplies another example of wrongheadedness, if one may use so harsh a word, in the manly and winning revelation of a conflict between his natural instincts and his formal creed:

> Certainly I must confess my own barbarousness, I never heard the old song of Percy and Douglas that I found not my heart moved more than with a trumpet, and yet is it sung but by some blind crowder, with no rougher voice than rude style; which, being so evil appareled in the dust and cobwebs of that uncivil age, what would it work, trimmed in the gorgeous eloquence of Pindar?

One danger in Renaissance classicism—especially as the art of the poet was associated with that of the orator—was a tendency to forget that style and form are inward and integral elements of writing, not a rhetorical vesture and pattern imposed from without; but this was a weakness of minor rather than major writers. More special diseases came out in the kind of verbal and rhetorical rash represented by such labels as Petrarchianism, Euphuism, Gongorism, and Marinism, and

1. Lionel Trilling, *Matthew Arnold* (New York: Norton, 1939), p. 168.

even the greatest writers, from Shakespeare down, might be infected. Yet these excesses cannot simply be ascribed to ancient influence, and a fundamental—and ultimately success-ful—aim of neoclassicism was to curb eccentricity and achieve a rational, civilized norm of expression. The lengths to which neoclassical concern for stylistic decorum could go were epigrammatically summed up in George Brandes' re-mark about Voltaire, that the man who respected little in heaven or earth respected the uniform caesura.[2]

The formal literary creed of the Renaissance was an amal-gam of Aristotle and Horace and others, fused and reinter-preted by theorists and practitioners in terms of their own age and country. Although there was emphasis on the emo-tive power of poetry, the creed tended to operate on a practi-cal level, to convert suggestive principles into a code of rules. The most familiar example is the crystallization of Aristotle's basic doctrine of unity of dramatic action, along with his more casual reference to the customary limit of time, into the three unities of action, time, and place. The authority of the unities was not broken until the eighteenth century. But "the rules" were always much stronger in France, the Gallic mind being disposed toward order and decorum, than in England, where the national genius was not so disposed and where Shakespeare remained one powerful solvent. In Europe at large, it should be added, the hardening of the rules was at least checked by two perennial sources of fire, the Platonic conception of poetic "enthusiasm" and, in later phases, the treatise on the sublime that goes under the name of Longinus.

It was the formalistic habit of mind that translated or per-verted the Aristotelian doctrine of imitation of nature, of life, into imitation of ancient authors, whose imitations of life

2. George Brandes, *Main Currents in Nineteenth Century Literature* (London: Heinemann; New York: Macmillan, 1906), I, 3.

were by common consent the supreme models. This theory of literary imitation had, to be sure, originated in antiquity, but it remained a fairly moderate and judicious precept until the Renaissance made it a prime article in the neoclassical creed. It was expounded, for example, in Vida's *Art of Poetry* in the early sixteenth century and in Pope's *Essay on Criticism* in the early eighteenth. Virgil, says Pope, planned to draw the *Aeneid* wholly from nature,

> But when t' examine ev'ry part he came,
> Nature and Homer were, he found, the same.
> Convinc'd, amaz'd, he checks the bold design;
> And rules as strict his labour'd work confine,
> As if the Stagirite o'erlooked each line.
> Learn hence for ancient rules a just esteem;
> To copy Nature is to copy them.

Obviously such a theory was in danger of encouraging academic reproductions of the antique, not expressions of human experience. On the other hand, such a theory, wisely followed, inculcated a beneficial consciousness of great materials and great form and style; it meant that writers and readers were aware of tradition, of the principles of decorum governing the various genres, of controlling standards above individual vagaries and fashions of the moment.

Such ideas and attitudes are as far removed from those of our time as Renaissance education is, and they might disconcert a reader who was wholly conditioned by modern theory and practice. The modern writer cares nothing for genres and is likely to associate convention with stereotypes— although the reader of *Lycidas*, for instance, knows how greatly a great poet can work in and through a convention. The modern poet and reader assume that poetry must be written in the language and rhythms of common speech; the

Renaissance poet and reader would accept that doctrine for satire but would expect most other kinds of poetry to be distinctly poetical. The modern writer and reader, while abhorring didacticism, expect a poem to be a revelation of the author's state of mind, to be, that is, a disillusioned comment on life. The Renaissance writer and reader normally held a firm belief in the ethical function of poetry and at the same time wrote and treasured lovely pieces of jeweled artifice that told little about the poet and less about life; and in neither case was self-expression regarded as the end. These are a few rapid and unqualified contrasts, but they may serve their purpose.

We have noted some virtues of Renaissance education and literary theory and have admitted also the danger, for a writer, of overeducation—which is not the commonest danger in our time. An educated writer of the Renaissance, although he was a man living in his own world, having his own experience, could not simply look in his heart, or around him, and write. He was himself so eagerly responsive to literary tradition, and critical authority was so busy in the necessary task of ordering and refining form and style, that only an original mind could keep his balance. But if, for instance, we are deaf to the muffled sound and fury of the hundreds of academic Senecan dramas, the fashion may be said to have been justified by such a non-academic product as *Hamlet*. In other words, the greatest writers of the Renaissance were those who, granted their special genius, could profit from the classics without becoming sedulous apes and without losing their own fresh vision of life or their contact with native and popular elements of tradition.

That is doubtless a truism, but, for a varied array of illustrious examples, consider such men as Ariosto, Tasso, Camoens, Spenser, Rabelais, and Cervantes. The first four represent the heroic poem, which the Renaissance, in its general exaltation of classical genres, put at the top. Petrarch's unfinished but ambitiously cherished *Africa* was the first of the scores of neoclassical epics which were to litter the sixteenth, seventeenth, and eighteenth centuries and of which only one transcendent work survives, *Paradise Lost*. But the four poets just mentioned, although influenced by the classics, were not strict neoclassicists in method or style. Ariosto, going back to the romances of Charlemagne and chivalry, which Boiardo had lately handled, created a lively and brilliant panoramic narrative, at once idealistic and ironical. The Italian critics were much exercised over the question whether the *Orlando Furioso*, with its fluid episodic structure and numerous heroes and heroines, was an epic or a romance, but some reached the sage conclusion that, if Aristotle could have read it, he would have approved. Half a century later, at the time of Lepanto, the serious Tasso turned to the Crusades for material and, rendered more conscious of problems of form, made a more unified but still highly romantic poem. Spenser, hoping to "overgo" the Italians, and linking them as ethical teachers with Homer and Virgil, likewise used the materials of chivalry, folklore, and the supernatural, all informed by the desire to "fashion a gentleman or noble person in vertuous and gentle discipline." Spenser drew upon a wide range of ancient, medieval, and modern literature, Platonic and Aristotelian ethics, Ovid and Virgil, medieval romances and the Italian heroic poems. Finally, Camoens achieved success in what might have seemed an impossible feat; he made the relatively recent voyage of Vasco da Gama the theme of a Portuguese epic, with celestial machinery taken from classical myth. What gave life to these poems was not merely the use of national history or legend (which neoclassical theory and ancient practice prescribed), but originality, vigor, and eclecticism that went far beyond imitation. On the other hand Ronsard, the prince of sixteenth-century French lyrists, felt impelled to write a national epic, and declared, with unconscious irony, that, unless his readers knew the ancients well, his poem would be a dead weight in their hands. Like so many things of its kind, it was a dead weight anyhow.

As for the two great men of prose, Rabelais, a classical humanist and medical scientist, is no exemplar of neoclassical decorum; he carried the Paul Bunyanesque giant-lore of popular tradition to a new level of uproarious humor, satire, and *joie de vivre*. The more sober Cervantes can hardly, any more than Shakespeare, be grouped with scholarly writers—although a modern critic has remarked that his "discovery of Aristotle, even at second or third hand, with the revelation that literature had its own body of precept, its rules, was the great aesthetic experience of his life" [3]—but Cervantes was, like Shakespeare, a great interpreter of man who was not diverted from the popular by neoclassicism. On the other hand, we may think that Cervantes' profound sanity and irony, like Shakespeare's, would not be what they are if his age had not been tempered by classical rationality. At the same time, thinking of ancient comedy, we might add that other qualities in Cervantes and Shakespeare, the clear recognition of good and evil, the sympathetic understanding of human idealism and human folly, were possible only in a civilization leavened by Christianity.

In this general connection we cannot very well avoid the conventional, not to say threadbare, contrast between Shakespeare and Jonson, although Shakespeare was not the mere child of nature of many early eulogies and although Jonson

3. W. C. Atkinson, "Miguel de Cervantes," *Fortnightly Review* (November, 1947), p. 375.

was not a mere neoclassicist. When we compare their dramatizations of Roman history, it is obvious that Shakespeare exercised his untrammeled intuition upon the characters and data of North's *Plutarch* and heightened the vivid contemporaneous immediacy already present in the translation; whereas Jonson, with the historical conscience of a scholar, enveloped Sejanus and Catiline in speeches more studiously composed out of Cicero, Sallust, Tacitus, and scholarly commentaries. Jonson's powers found their chief expression of course in comedy, and here he had before him classical comedy and satire and the precepts of Horace and modern critics. Some of Shakespeare's romantic comedies had a remote classical ancestry, since pastoral romances of the Renaissance were derived from late Greek and medieval romance, but the world of Arden, Illyria, and Bohemia had little to do with relentless satire of urban manners and morals, of knaves and gulls.

There is a similar typical difference in the two poets' lyrics. Shakespeare's, although not naïve, have an air of spontaneous ease and a clear affinity with popular song—and so do some of Jonson's. But some of Jonson's most characteristic pieces, such as "Drink to me only with thine eyes," come from classical sources and show the conscious contrivance, the intellectualized pattern and style, of a scholarly poet. For example, take their handling of the ancient theme of *Carpe diem,* on which hundreds of Renaissance poets rang all possible changes over and over again. In "O mistress mine, where are you roaming?" the theme is classical and its development is strictly logical, but we forget all that in hearing a simple, innocent, tuneful ditty from a timeless Arcadia. As soon as we begin Jonson's

Come, my Celia, let us prove,
While we may, the sports of love,

we know that we are intended to enjoy a light adaptation of Catullus, a picture of the sophisticated game of love as played in ancient Rome or modern London. But all these obvious remarks are by way of distinction, not disparagement of the lesser poet. Jonson was much too fine an artist, and much too tough-minded an observer of life, to reveal more than traces of the pedantry of neoclassicism. For him, as for other independent writers, the ancients were "Guides, not Commanders."

We may turn to one or two representative classical themes which were treated in lyric and heroic poem, in prose tale and drama. None was more central in the tradition than the story of Troy, and none illustrates better the infinite poetic value of a malleable body of myth that is a universal inheritance. A modern poet who wished to deal with the subject would read Homer, in translation. Some Renaissance poets knew Greek, and all knew the Trojan parts of Virgil and Ovid, but many used, and few were unaffected by, the very un-Homeric mixture of epic and romance that the Middle Ages built upon a rough ancient foundation. Every student of literature, or at least every candidate for the Ph.D., knows the outline of the long process that began with the prosaic and circumstantial narratives of Dares and Dictys, the medieval substitutes for Homer. The large and romantic elaborations of these tales were not products of "medieval naïveté"; they were sophisticated modernizations of the kind begun by Ovid, the chief progenitor of courtly love, and often written in our time. For Englishmen of the Elizabethan age the standard popular version of the Trojan story was the prose romance translated from the French by Caxton, a version which, by the way, continued to be printed up into the eighteenth century.

One offshoot of this tradition became, especially in England, almost as conspicuous as the parent stem, that is, the wholly medieval story of Troilus, Cressida, and Diomede. The story was first developed in the Old French *Romance of Troy*, of the twelfth century, and was widely known through the Latin prose version of that work. It was expanded by Boccaccio, who drew upon his own experience as well as literary sources. Following Boccaccio, Chaucer recreated the characters and their significance with all his own humor, dramatic power, sympathetic insight, and tragic irony. The world of his great poem or novel of courtly love is of course not Homeric but chivalric; Chaucer's vision of realities was not obstructed by a concern for archaeology. Then the Scottish Chaucerian, Robert Henryson, wrote a short and moving sequel in which the faithless Cressida sank to painful degradation; in the sixteenth century this poem was commonly read as Chaucer's, and it had a large share in fixing the popular notion of the heroine. Finally Shakespeare, whether experiencing a dark mood of cynicism or experimenting in the acrid Jonsonian vein of satire, made his dramatic version in which traditional ideals of love and honor are corroded by the poisons of "war and lechery." We need not go on to Dryden's play.

This brief sketch is a reminder that the classical revival did not mean that Renaissance writers and readers outlawed pseudo-classical inventions and intermediaries and gave themselves exclusively to the authentic classics. There was no reason why they should have done so, since the themes of literature are not a matter of historical purism and ancient literature itself had been a long series of similar accretions and variations. One side of this question must have a word more. Recent scholarship has been revealing to what an unexpected—and yet altogether natural—degree even learned writers of the Renaissance made use of dictionaries of mythology, a practice that to some people may carry a suggestion of the second-hand and cheap. But, since all poets had some classical education and a feeling for antiquity, it made small difference where an immediate hint came from. And the importance of handbooks of myth, such as those of Boccaccio and Natalis Comes and Cartari, was not merely that they fulfilled the function of similar modern books, but still more that they gave allegorical and ethical interpretations. It was no less legitimate and fruitful, for such well-educated poets as Spenser and Chapman and even the learned Jonson, to use such works than it was for Mr. Eliot to use *The Golden Bough.*

Wherever poets got their inspiration, it was, as I said before, of immeasurable value that they and their readers should share a traditional, international, and inexhaustibly varied treasury of myth and symbol. Such symbols could become meaningless counters, but they have always been fresh when felt freshly. For one famous, simple, and magical example, that slangy Elizabethan journalist, Thomas Nashe, could create such an atmosphere that one name calls up all the associations of glamorous youth and beauty and love, and age and death:

> Beauty is but a flower
> Which wrinkles will devour;
> Brightness falls from the air,
> Queens have died young and fair,
> Dust hath closed Helen's eye.
> I am sick, I must die.
>   Lord, have mercy on us!

And with that must be linked a no less familiar and magical evocation:

> Was this the face that launched a thousand ships,

The Classics and Imaginative Literature

And burnt the topless towers of Ilium?
Sweet Helen, make me immortal with a kiss.

If we ask why—apart from the poets' expressive power—
these classical allusions are so moving, one answer is that they
crystallize the conflict between paganism and medieval Christianity. Nashe, in the time of the plague, sees the most beautiful of women against the background of *"Ubi sunt . . . ?"*
and the Dance of Death. And neither Dr. Faustus, the very
symbol of Renaissance *hubris*, nor Marlowe, who has often
been called that, can escape from God. Faustus' vision of an
immortality of the senses is a contrivance of the devil; and
later, when he must surrender his soul and time will not stand
still, his delusive ecstasy is recalled by the use of the Ovidian
Aurora's cry to the horses of the night to check their gallop
and prolong her joys. But then his agonized vision is of
Christ's blood streaming in the firmament, God's ireful brows,
and immortality in hell.

Classical myth was not always treated with such poignant
brevity. But we shall pass by the innumerable and richly
decorative versions of myths and tales which were written in
Italy, France, Spain, and England, and of which the best-
known specimens are *Hero and Leander* and *Venus and
Adonis*. In such poems the sensuous or the sensual might be
an end in itself, or it might embody a philosophic theme. The
same thing may be said of the mythological allusions which
are everywhere in Renaissance writing. Ovid's *Metamorphoses*, the most popular ancient storehouse of both tales and
allusions, was itself highly pictorial. Renaissance poets, led by
the Italians, went far beyond Ovid, and beyond medieval
Ovidians like Chaucer, in pictorial elaboration and sensuous
warmth and color. One general reason, amply illustrated in
contemporary Italian painting, was a new, and what used to

be called "pagan," recognition of the beauties of art and nature and the human body. A weighty theoretical sanction was provided by the doctrine *"ut pictura poesis."* This doctrine, originally a compound of ideas and phrases from Simonides, Aristotle, Horace, and Plutarch, made poetry a speaking picture and painting silent poetry. That is, a poet should with words create the effect of the painter's brush and pigments. To poets rediscovering the world of the senses, it was a congenial creed, and it lasted up to Lessing and beyond. To take one example, Ovid, describing the pictures woven by Arachne, says simply that "she made Leda lying under the wings of the swan." Spenser, describing the tapestries in the house of Busyrane, gives a whole stanza to the scene:

> Then was he turnd into a snowy Swan,
>   To win faire Leda to his lovely trade:
>   O wondrous skill, and sweet wit of the man,
>   That her in daffadillies sleeping made,
>   From scorching heat her daintie limbes to shade:
>   Whiles the proud Bird ruffing his fethers wyde,
>   And brushing his faire brest, did her invade;
>   She slept, yet twixt her eyelids closely spyde,
> How towards her he rusht, and smiled at his pryde.

The doctrine *"ut pictura poesis"* could of course encourage description for the sake of description, but the stanza quoted, like almost all such things in the most pictorial of poets, has a purpose; Spenser is illustrating, with appropriate "realism," the sensual attractions of courtly love.

One special and popular convention was the catalogue of the beauties of the female body. Here again there is a contrast between the medieval catalogue, comprehensive but cool, and the Renaissance catalogue, comprehensive and warm. This sort of description, starting from the Song of Songs, Anac-

34

reon, and Ovid, had an influential exponent in Ariosto, in his pictures of the sensual enchantress Alcina and of Angelica and Olympia, who were both, like Andromeda, bound naked to a rock. Among English poets who took over the convention were Thomas Watson (who named Ariosto as one of the sources of his "passion"), Sir Philip Sidney, and Spenser. Spenser, in the *Amoretti* and *Epithalamion,* raised the tone of such catalogues above mere lusciousness. The *Epithalamion,* the finest love poem in the language, is an example of Spenser's eclectic yet wholly individual quality. It is a wedding hymn in the tradition of Catullus and other Roman poets and their French imitators, in the form of a stately Italian canzone, a series of processional pictures with a mingling of realistic and mythological allusions, of Irish and Roman festivities, all wrought into a ritualistic offering worthy of the Christian marriage altar.

While Ovidian narratives and anatomical catalogues were outlets for neopaganism, Renaissance poets could be quite sincere and serious in using a similar technique to depict sensual temptation as the insidious foe of man's integrity and the heroic life. The great vehicle for that theme was inevitably the story of Circe. The moral implicit in Homer was recognized in antiquity and was made very explicit by such Renaissance interpreters of myth as Natalis Comes. In Renaissance poetry Circe's sisters and cousins, if not aunts, may be reckoned by the dozens. Even the light-hearted Ariosto, although normally no moralist, made Alcina's powers of seduction the occasion of a moral episode. Tasso's Armida and the luxurious sensuality of her abode gave some materials and ideas to Spenser, whose Bower of Bliss is for most of us the great example of the tradition. But the climax of Spenser's book of Temperance was far from a mere imitation of Tasso, partly because he fused together a varied abundance of related motifs, Homeric, medieval, and Italian, and still more because he made every item in the account of the Bower and its inmates contribute to the cumulative and overpowering picture of debilitated lust. Critics have often gone wrong about the Bower of Bliss, saying that for once the serious moralist has broken out of harness and let himself go in satisfying his essentially voluptuous temperament. But, since C. S. Lewis wrote on Spenser,[4] no one can fall into that error again. The poet followed two main lines of suggestion. One is emphasis on his favorite contrast between rich unwholesome artifice and simple healthy nature. Ivy, for instance, is made of gold colored to imitate real ivy, and even its branches partake of the character of the Bower—"Low his lascivious armes adown did creepe." The second line of suggestion is emphasis on the diseased sensuality which enjoys only the perpetual and unsated lust of the eye—represented by the strip-tease damsels in the pool and by the Circean Acrasia—as opposed to the healthy, honorable love and fruition symbolized in the Garden of Adonis and especially in the representative of chastity and true love, Britomart. In contrast with the natural health of the Garden, or Britomart's passionate love for her future husband, the atmosphere of Acrasia's Bower is heavy with corruption. If, by the way, we think of Spenser's characteristic diffuseness as very far from classical conciseness (or from the elliptical conciseness of parallel episodes in *The Waste Land*), we should ask if his desired effects could have been achieved without aggregation and repetition.

This topic has brought us within reach of the last thing we can discuss, the conflict, in and behind much serious Renaissance literature, between orthodox Christian humanism and the rising forces of scepticism and naturalism. That conflict is

4. C. S. Lewis, *The Allegory of Love* (Oxford University Press, 1938), chap. vii.

at the center of our subject because the classics gave powerful support to both sides—and, in somewhat altered terms, the conflict is still with us.

The modern phrase "Christian humanism" is a label for the medieval and Renaissance synthesis, the result of the long effort, which began with some of the Church Fathers, to reconcile and fuse the natural wisdom of the pagans with the supernatural illumination of Christianity. The first great philosophic system, that of Aquinas, rested on the poles of divine and human reason. The Thomistic synthesis, however, gave way to the voluntarism, represented by William of Ockham, which made God not Absolute Reason but Absolute Will, a concept which passed on to Luther and Calvin, with all the added force of the Augustinian doctrine of human depravity. The Christian humanists of the Renaissance were more literary and practical, and less rigorously philosophical, than the scholastics, and their ideal was the religion of the New Testament instead of scholastic logic, but they may be said to have inherited something of the Thomistic impulse and attitude. The Renaissance philosophy of order, although not a *summa* built by any one mind, was a reassertion of the rationality of God and the rational dignity and free will of man —hence, for example, Erasmus' break with Luther. This mode of thought, or view of life, attained its most coherent maturity in the seventeenth century, with Milton and the Cambridge Platonists, but most essentials were set forth in the first book of Hooker's *Ecclesiastical Polity*, where he surveyed the reign of law in the universe and in the mind of God and man.

This philosophy of order has been described rather often of late years, and only a few headings can be recalled now. The center and foundation was of course Christian faith and theology, with its conception of God and the nature and destiny of man. Then the whole universe, from God down to inanimate nature, is a hierarchy of being. It is the glory, and the peril, of man that he occupies a middle position, linked on the one hand with the angels and God, on the other with the beasts. He is endowed with a rational soul, which should rule over his appetites and passions as God rules over the forces of nature. What holds for the universe and the individual also holds for society, which is not a chaotic aggregate of individuals but a hierarchical organism in which everyone has his place and function. Thus the individual soul and society and the cosmos constitute one interrelated order. Perhaps the briefest and most eloquent summary is the sentence with which Hooker closes his first book:

> . . . Of Law there can be no less acknowledged, than that her seat is the bosom of God, her voice the harmony of the world: all things in heaven and earth do her homage, the very least as feeling her care, and the greatest as not exempted from her power, both angels and men and creatures of what condition soever, though each in different sort and manner, yet all with uniform consent, admiring her as the mother of their peace and joy.

There is no time to show how ethical, social, and metaphysical components of this doctrine were drawn from Aristotle, from Plato and Neoplatonism, and from the Stoicism of Cicero and Seneca. Nor is there time for more than one or two references to the way in which it conditioned or worked in imaginative literature. The *locus classicus* for some things is Ulysses' speech on "degree" in *Troilus and Cressida*, a speech which has been related to Hooker and to Sir Thomas Elyot's *Governor* and which is at any rate good humanistic orthodoxy. But it is only one small and concrete illustration of the fact that the orthodox synthesis provided the underlying assumptions of Shakespeare's plays. If that assertion seems disputable, we have only to put him beside some modern naturalistic writers to realize that his characters speak, act, and are judged in relation to a philosophy of order and are not merely observed with entire moral detachment or in a moral vacuum.

For more tangible evidence, we may glance at a poet and dramatist who, unlike Shakespeare, was an earnest crusader and, in a not altogether pejorative sense, a doctrinaire preacher. George Chapman's large borrowings, which he fused into a creed both typically humanistic and intensely personal, have been laid bare by scholarship, and the names of some principal creditors are significant—Epictetus, Plutarch, Marsilio Ficino, Erasmus, Natalis Comes.[5] In other words, Chapman is a Christian Stoic with a marked strain of Platonism. In his central poem, *The Tears of Peace*, Chapman urges men to translate learning into active moral wisdom, the reason's control of the body's mutinous realm; that is "the rich crown of old Humanity." His tragedies about Bussy d'Ambois and Byron are dramatic presentations of passion and will running amuck, in contrast with the disciplined insight and self-control of the "Senecal man." Even in his noble version of Homer, whom he worshiped as the supreme poet and teacher, Chapman continually made explicit, sometimes with considerable additions to the text, the same conflict between reason and passion. I am rather given to quoting, from Chapman's preface to the *Odyssey*, a piece of fervent and eloquent Stoicism in which he is comparing Achilles with his great hero, Odysseus:

In one, predominant perturbation; in the other, overruling wisdom; in one, the body's fervor and fashion of outward

5. Franck L. Schoell, *Études sur l'humanisme continental en Angleterre* (Paris: H. Champion, 1926).

fortitude to all possible height of heroical action; in the other, the mind's inward, constant, and unconquered empire, unbroken, unaltered, with any most insolent and tyrannous infliction.

That was the spirit in which Homer could be read, and we could hardly have more impressive testimony to reverence for ancient greatness and to the ethical function of poetry.

In England this philosophy of order commanded almost complete allegiance. Among writers, there was only an occasional rebel like the young John Donne, who in religion was not a sceptic (in the sense of unbeliever) but who in some moods enjoyed making witty and paradoxical arguments for sexual promiscuity. On the continent both religious scepticism and ethical naturalism had long been rising in strength; indeed these modes of thought were as old as their humanistic opposites, or older. Whereas Christian humanism carried on, from Plato and others, a belief in universal values sanctioned alike by God and by nature, God's instrument, scepticism, whether deistic or more radical, denied the Christian scheme, and naturalism, appealing to a different conception of "nature," denied the moral absolutes of classical and Christian thought. Even Cicero, the chief source of Renaissance humanism, was also, through his books on the nature of the gods and on divination, a source of sceptical and naturalistic arguments, which were used, for instance, by Rabelais and Montaigne. Other ancient solvents of orthodoxy were Lucretius, the passionate preacher of Epicurean materialism; Pliny, who acknowledged no God except Nature and saw man as inferior to animals in the struggle for survival; Lucian, the arch-mocker of all things sacrosanct; and Sextus Empiricus, who expounded the Pyrrhonist doctrine of the impossibility of knowledge. The Middle Ages contributed much to these streams of thought—Averroistic pantheism, Nominalism, which drove a wedge between reason and faith and rejected universal abstractions in favor of the particulars of experience, and the libertine naturalism of such men as Jean de Meun, the second author of the immensely popular *Romance of the Rose*. From the early sixteenth century onward, the "Aristotelian" rationalism of Pomponazzi gained ground in Italy and spread from there to France. Even the Reformation, as the first great rebellion against religious authority, gave aid and comfort to much more thoroughgoing rebels.

As one representative of scepticism and naturalism we may take the first and greatest of modern essayists, Montaigne. When he began his serious reading and writing, secluded in that tower of his château which rose above household bustle, Montaigne's search for an ethical philosophy led him in the Stoic direction. But a man so responsive to life, so curious about human and especially his own nature, could not dwell for long on the plane of Senecan austerity. The influence of the more practical and flexible Plutarch, the awakening of his instinctive independence, and the discovery of Sextus Empiricus brought him to a second phase, represented by the "Apology of Raymond Sebond." This long essay, far from being a defense of natural theology, turns into an exposition of Pyrrhonist scepticism, a denial of the claims of the senses and reason to attain truth and of the possibility of human communication with ultimate reality. But such scepticism was for Montaigne less of a weapon than a broom, a means of clearing the way to a working creed of relativism and naturalism. The Stoic maxim, "Follow Nature," which meant allying one's self with the collective "right reason" of mankind and the providential course of the world, he translates into "Follow your own nature." Man cannot, says Montaigne, rise above himself (as Seneca had urged), except through religion, and, although always a nominal Catholic, he does not take much personal account of divine grace; he has neither an angel's nor a horse's conscience but a man's conscience, which is contented with itself. There were higher levels than that, and lower ones. Montaigne's was a discriminating and, up to a point, a fastidious nature which required intellectual and philosophic pleasures, and in his own way he was inclined toward order and tradition; for him, Alexander, who conquered the world, was a lesser man than Socrates, who led his life in conformity with nature—although Socrates might not have found Montaigne's creed quite satisfying. Thus Montaigne's influence was to support both conservatism and sceptical naturalism. He has been mentioned here as a supremely candid and disturbing questioner of accepted verities and pseudo-verities, who leaves aspiring man stripped, for good or ill, of many of his traditional supports and ideals.

These two antagonistic conceptions of life, both in a large degree classical, bring us into the modern world with all its conflicts and confusions, which since 1600 have been greatly heightened by science. We must stop here, although I should like to have mentioned other things. There are, for example, Spenser's *Cantos of Mutability*, in which the poet rises far above his Ovidian materials to present, or rather to admit, the painful struggle between his belief in a world evolving under divine providence and his vivid consciousness of a world of cruel strife and change. But to end with Shakespeare, as no doubt we should, we may say that by the time of the great tragedies the finest of minds, grown restless and sceptical, is able to question traditional beliefs, to entertain the idea of life as meaningless flux, and to probe the depths of evil, and yet he has not lost the traditional ideal of inward and outward order and faith in the actual or potential greatness and goodness of man.

The Classics and Imaginative Literature

Thus the briefest sketch of classical influence in Renaissance literature becomes a picture, not of a well quietly filling up with literary culture, but of many vigorous currents and whirlpools, literary and philosophical, scientific and religious. And one of many paradoxes is that the age which in literature and thought was zealously seeking order was also the age that saw the rise of modern naturalism. The naturalistic creed is now the natural creed of modern minds, who insist that no other view of life is possible—although we seem to hear less of the moral wisdom evolved by that creed than of laments for the breakdown of values. At any rate, however disheartening the spectacle of our civilization, the classics are still there as both a dynamic and a stabilizing force, and some of the chief writers of our century are proof of the continued vitality of the classical tradition.

III

English Poetry:
God and Nature

Thirty years ago Merritt Hughes described what he called "The Kidnapping of Donne"—that is, the ways in which the ardor of discovery led many of the literati to take Donne out of the past and make him over in the likeness of a modern intellectual. He was seen as an emancipated sceptic and rebel, boldly and intensely absorbed in his own experience, cut off by rationalistic and scientific sophistication from traditional roots and beliefs, and alienated from the current orthodoxies of his world. This distortion of the real Donne is an example of what happens when critics and readers take an unhistorical shortcut. But, even though during this last generation many students of the history of ideas have put Donne and other poets—Spenser, Shakespeare, Milton, and lesser men—in a much richer and clearer historical setting, and thereby enlightened our comprehension of their minds and writings, we may still be disposed to give the highest marks to those writers who sound or can be made to sound modern. If, on the contrary, we lack such confidence in the criterion of modernity, it might be better, when we read and assess great poets of the past, if we ask what they would think of us, since their scale of values may be less in need of readjustment than our own. In these two lectures I should like to recall some of the religious, metaphysical, and ethical premises which were almost universal in their age and which are far removed from the naturalistic outlook that now is almost universal.

Observations and illustrations—the latter drawn from the most familiar poems and plays—may be grouped under four spacious headings, God, Nature, Time, and Man. These cannot really be separated from one another, but they will serve our turn. We are concerned with the orthodoxy that even the most sophisticated writers commonly shared with their public, and we do not need to take much account of anti-Christian scepticism or deism or atheism. Although such modes of thought had gained considerable headway in Italy and France, they apparently had not in England; English writing contains many horrified denunciations of irreligion, but that is about all we find. We may think of the charges brought against Marlowe, and yet, whatever his private convictions, his plays are somewhat doubtful evidence, and *Doctor Faustus*, if we knew nothing of its author, might stand as the most positively Christian of Elizabethan tragedies. Similar charges were brought against Sir Walter Ralegh, but, as Ernest A. Strathmann has shown, Ralegh was quite orthodox; his *History of the World*, as no reader can fail to see, was founded on the theme of God's providence working itself out in the rise and fall of empires. As for Donne, who has often been called a sceptic by modern critics, there is no evidence that he ever entertained the slightest doubt of the articles of Christian faith. It is not until the middle third of the seventeenth cen-

45

tury that we come to an English writer, such as Hobbes, who can be thought of as irreligious, and even Hobbes is not openly so; he may indeed have considered himself a good Christian. To say all this is not of course to say that all Renaissance Englishmen thought and acted with exemplary piety and virtue; they had all the passions and vices of men in general, and in a high degree, but they had not cast off the religious view of sin and did not think of wickedness as merely antisocial behavior.

To come to our first heading, and to understand the place of reason in classical-Christian thought of the Renaissance, we have to begin where so many things begin, with Plato and Aristotle. Whitehead's remark, that the European philosophical tradition consists of a series of footnotes to Plato, holds true in spite of what has been regarded as the long reign of Aristotle. Some factors that made Plato especially congenial to Christianity were his religious temper, his conception of God and righteousness and immortality, his positing of ideal absolutes above the world of appearance, and his belief that man could, through intellectual, ethical, and spiritual discipline, attain comprehension of those absolutes. Plato's conviction that the true philosopher must be like God could be readily translated into the imitation of Christ. The assimilation of Neoplatonism by Christianity can only be mentioned. Although during the Middle Ages very little of Plato was directly known to the West, a good deal of Platonism was transmitted through Cicero and Augustine and Boethius, as well as through the more recalcitrant medium of Aristotle. And during the Renaissance "Platonism" was a mixture of Plato and his interpreters, ancient, medieval, and modern. Aristotle was of course the great classical and rational element in the so-called medieval synthesis of Thomas Aquinas. In that synthesis, the world was seen as the rational creation of a rational God which man could comprehend, up to a point, through his divine gift of reason; beyond that point, revelation must supply the supra-rational truths essential for salvation.

But this synthesis had hardly been formulated before it began to break up. In later scholastic thought the Thomistic conception of God as Intelligent Being gave way to the conception of God as Will. Man's reason no longer kept him, so to speak, a collaborator with an intelligible God; instead, both Creator and creature were removed from the realm of reason to the realm of faith, a shift which exalted the power of God at the expense of the rational dignity of man. From this cleavage between reason and faith two divergent tendencies developed. One, greatly assisted by the Renaissance revival of ancient scepticism, was anti-Christian rationalism. The other development was the theology of Luther and Calvin, which set a gulf between the absolute and inscrutable sovereignty of God and the depravity of man, who was impotent without the gift, the arbitrary gift, of grace.

The antagonism between Luther and Erasmus was much like that between Augustine and Pelagius a thousand years earlier. Erasmus, the Christian humanist *par excellence*, insisted on man's free will and rational power of choice and capacity for good, on simple practice of "the philosophy of Christ." The imitation of Christ was the end of life and education. Erasmus was more widely read throughout Europe than perhaps any other writer in history except Cicero, and he had enormous influence. In his constant pleas for piety and culture Erasmus constantly quoted Plato and Cicero. In a moving comment on a moving passage in Cicero he says that there may be more saints than the church takes account of, and he echoes the liturgy, "Sancte Socrates, ora pro nobis." That famous and infinitely suggestive phrase explains why

47

Christian humanists appealed to the classics as the handmaids of Christian faith and virtue. Such high-minded pagans as Plato and Cicero and Seneca, by the light of natural reason (itself a gift bestowed by God on all men alike), approached the threshold of Christianity, and their moral wisdom was a persuasive and practical supplement to the teachings of Christ. This ideal of rational and cultivated piety, of virtue and good letters, was carried on in various ways—to speak only of England—by such humanists as the Platonic Sir Thomas Elyot, Roger Ascham, and others, even John Lyly—I say "even" because the style of *Euphues* may obscure a modern reader's recognition of the traditional ideals.

Those ideals were more ethical and practical, more literary, and less philosophical, than the Thomistic synthesis had been, and for that reason were more readily understood and assimilated. The Tudor humanists upheld the necessity of classical wisdom along with the Bible. Luther and Calvin could on occasion quote the classics, but the whole force of their doctrines was opposed to any such fusion of the natural reason with faith. And the doctrines of the Elizabethan Church of England were Calvinistic; it was not until the early seventeenth century that the Church moved away from Calvinism. Here we must glance at the great Elizabethan and Protestant restatement of the Thomistic synthesis, Richard Hooker's *Of the Laws of Ecclesiastical Polity* (1593). Hooker's immediate motive was a defense of the Church of England against the Puritan ideal of an apostolic simplicity in church government; but Hooker's largeness of mind raised his work far above the polemical plane, so that his name is coupled with Burke's as a symbol of rational order and tradition.

For our purpose, the difference between Hooker's Christian humanism and Calvinistic doctrine may be illustrated by one assertion, an assertion which, coming from a devout Christian, may at first sight appear startling:

> The general and perpetual voice of men is as the sentence
> of God himself. For that which all men have at all times
> learned, Nature herself must needs have taught; and God
> being the author of Nature, her voice is but his instrument.

For Hooker, as for Aquinas or any Christian, revelation
alone contains the truths necessary for salvation. But the
physical and the moral universe constitutes a rational order,
under the reign of divine and natural law. Man's God-given
reason enables him to comprehend the nature of that order
and to cooperate with it. Hooker is invoking the long tradition of "right reason" which rational Christianity had inherited from ancient Stoicism: absolutes exist, not merely
because they are revealed in the Bible, but because they
have been recognized by the natural reason, the collective
wisdom, of mankind. These absolute values man has seen
in the nature of things, and God himself, if he could be
imagined as having the wish to alter them, could not do so.
This view of rational order and law is at the opposite pole
from Calvinism. Calvin and his followers say that there are
no such absolutes, that nothing is in itself reasonable and
just: whatever God wills thereupon becomes reasonable and
just.

We may seem to be keeping away from the literature of the
English Renaissance, but actually we are not. It has often been
argued that Shakespeare, in set speeches on the theme of order,
notably that of Ulysses in *Troilus and Cressida*, embodies
direct echoes of Elyot and Hooker. However that may be,
the conception of a divine and rational order is the background and foundation of serious Elizabethan and Jacobean
literature, whether it is expounded or assumed or, at times,
questioned or ignored. Not everyone read Hooker, but the

general creed, in more elementary and popular forms, was established before 1593. This creed has been made so familiar, by Dr. Tillyard and other scholars, that we do not need to linger over it, except to emphasize its central importance and to recall a few main articles. We have observed one, the concept of right reason, the eternal law of God and nature written, as Cicero said, in every human heart. Another is that of the great chain of being, the hierarchical order of creation which descends from the Creator through angels and man to animals and plants and stones. This order at once distinguishes and unites all levels of existence, all creatures and all things, the concrete and the abstract. The hierarchical order of the creation is, or should be, reproduced in society, in which all men have their due place and function. It operates, or should operate, in the soul of man: in terms of Plato's ethical psychology, reason should control man's appetites and passions as God controls the physical world. This all-embracing view of God, the world, society, and man was to be increasingly shaken and finally undermined by various kinds of scepticism, but, as I have said, it met little direct opposition in sixteenth-century England. For most writers, including Shakespeare, it provided a generally accepted scale of values, a norm and criterion for the measurement of man's humanity and of social stability. No matter how far the great writers, from Shakespeare down, may have transcended this simple, unifying creed, the creed was there, a major premise and a bond of solidarity between writer and reader as well as in society at large. The writer, and in a special way the dramatist who wrote to be heard, could rely securely upon the religious and ethical reactions of his audience. There is a gulf between that situation and our world, a world which it has become fashionable to call post-Christian, and a world in which there may be only vestigial bonds among writers and between writers and readers.

For some philosophic minds, such as Hooker's, the conception of God might gather into itself elements of Plato or Aristotle, but for most people he was simply the God of traditional popular Christianity. It might be said, and with truth, that Elizabethan Christianity was Fundamentalist, yet that word, while it suggests the concrete and dramatic, would introduce a wrong atmosphere, a wrong set of associations. There is no need to outline traditional theology, which embraces everything, God and nature and time and man and earthly life and heaven and hell. But we must put aside the modern naturalistic view of a world of unknown origin and unknown destiny, a world containing nothing but physical and chemical substances and forces, among them the compound called man. Instead we must transport ourselves into a world which, with all its mundane activity and color, is the scene and battleground of supernatural agencies, God and his good angels opposing Satan and his evil spirits. It is a part of the divine scheme, and a consequence of the fall, that evil should exist, and that man, in himself and moved by impulses from above or below, should incline in one way or the other; he is not merely on his own. As various scholars have said, the archetypal pattern of the morality play, which is so obvious in Marlowe's *Doctor Faustus*, has left traces in Shakespeare. Macbeth is not simply a man led by ambition into crimes against his king and his fellows; he leagues himself with the agents of darkness and is ultimately overthrown by the agents of good. Malcolm, about to lead an army against the great criminal, can declare that

> the pow'rs above
> Put on their instruments.

For religious motives in general, it is enough to remember that

Shakespeare's most intellectual hero can talk with his father's ghost, be uncertain whether it is a good or an evil spirit (although it cannot injure his immortal soul), fear what might follow self-slaughter, and refrain from killing Claudius at prayer lest his victim go to heaven. And Hamlet can declare that

> There's a divinity that shapes our ends,
> Rough-hew them how we will,

that "there's a special providence in the fall of a sparrow." He pronounces it the will of heaven that he should have stabbed Polonius, that he should be God's scourge and minister; and heaven was ordinant even in enabling him to procure the death of Rosencrantz and Guildenstern instead of his own.

The Calvinistic God is often thought of in modern times as an irresponsible and terrifying Jehovah, a kind of Devil, and of course Calvinism had its grim and horrible aspects, as Robert Burton made very clear in his account of religious melancholy, of the despair and insanity that could be caused by fear of damnation. But Calvinistic doctrines, like other doctrines, could be held in different ways by people of different temperaments, and no one would suggest that the mass of Elizabethans suffered from the religious horrors. One great alleviation is brought up in one of the most vividly dramatic passages in *The Faerie Queene,* canto 9 of Book I. Here the Red Cross Knight, overcome by the consciousness of his sins, encounters the figure of Despair, who urges him to seek relief in suicide. The arguments of Despair, inconsistent but powerful, build up an overwhelming picture of God's rigorous and inflexible justice, and along with that a seductive picture of the sweetness of death. Red Cross is about to kill himself when Una snatches the knife from his hand and, for the only time, upbraids him:

> Come, come away, fraile, feeble, fleshly wight,
>   Ne let vaine words bewitch thy manly hart,
>   Ne divelish thoughts dismay thy constant spright.
>   In heavenly mercies hast thou not a part?
>   Why shouldst thou then despeire, that chosen art?
>   Where justice growes, there grows eke greater grace . . .

The assurance of divine love and mercy, which mitigates the terrors of death and hell, is invoked in the most diverse contexts, dramatic and personal. Spenser, after writing two more or less Platonic hymns to earthly love and beauty, turns to their heavenly counterparts, and we expect something more Platonic than we get. His third hymn is an almost purely evangelical celebration of Christ's love and life and death:

> O blessed well of love, O floure of grace,
> O glorious Morning starre, O lampe of light,
> Most lively image of thy fathers face,
> Eternall King of glorie, Lord of might,
> Meeke lambe of God before all worlds behight,
> How can we thee requite for all this good?
> Or what can prize that thy most precious blood?

Shakespeare, who has been called a Calvinist and a Catholic and a great heathen, puts the theme into two and a half lines uttered by Isabella in *Measure for Measure:*

>   Alas, alas!
> Why, all the souls that were were forfeit once,
> And he that might the vantage best have took
> Found out the remedy.

Marlowe's Faustus, in his last moments of despair, has no Una beside him, and he sees, but cannot yield to, a vision of redeeming love:

The stars move still, time runs, the clock will strike,
The devil will come, and Faustus must be damn'd.
O, I'll leap up to my God!—Who pulls me down?—
See, see, where Christ's blood streams in the firmament!
One drop would save my soul, half a drop: ah, my Christ!
Ah, rend not my heart for naming of my Christ!
Yet will I call on him: O, spare me, Lucifer!—
Where is it now? 'tis gone: and see, where God
Stretcheth out his arm, and bends his ireful brows!
Mountains and hills, come, come, and fall on me,
And hide me from the heavy wrath of God!

To turn to a sort of Faustus of real life, a man with a hydroptic thirst for learning and a restless mind, John Donne, as I remarked before, apparently never, in either his Catholic or his Anglican period, had any doubt of the Christian faith, but he could, looking back on his sins and forward to death and judgment, endure agonies of despair. In most of his sonnets, which nowadays are too familiar to quote, the universal and terrible drama is enacted on the lurid stage of Donne's imagination, and yet, while fear shakes his every joint, he can appeal to the promise of mercy and grace. Although individual consciences differed widely in sensitivity, there was a climate created by the belief that God is a party to, and judge of, man's every thought and act.

To come to our second heading, we ourselves in the twentieth century may be said to have five principal relations with nature, with the physical world. First, we owe to nature much of our food, a perhaps diminishing amount of our drink, and our clothing and shelter. Secondly, we suffer from the destructive forces of nature, storms, floods, and earthquakes. Thirdly, we enjoy the beauty of natural scenery, when we escape from pavements, buildings, and smog. Fourthly, there is the nature whose constituents and processes we know, or can know, from the investigations of science. Fifthly, there are the energies of nature that science and technology have more or less conquered, in Bacon's phrase, for the use and benefit of man's life.

The first three of these relations with nature were shared by the Elizabethans, and in some respects much more fully and closely. Elizabethan England had only one large city, and even it was not large by modern standards. The mass of people were much more directly dependent on the fruits of the earth and much more exposed to nature's destructiveness, and their senses and their lives were much more bound up with the scenes and the life of nature. We are so accustomed to our urban and industrial civilization that we may forget how recent and radical a phenomenon it is. Unless we have traveled in rather remote places we cannot easily imagine a mainly agricultural and pastoral world which in most essentials of work and play had not changed greatly since classical or biblical times. Virgil's *Georgics* could be read, with minor revisions, as a picture of Elizabethan yeoman life. The old seasonal customs, half-Christian, half-pagan (such as still survived in Hardy's Wessex), were both religious and festive bonds with nature. Mining and farming and manufacturing were beginning to be conducted on a large scale, but only beginning. Communities and households still retained a large measure of self-sufficiency. Travel was chiefly for the well-to-do; others stayed at home or, like beggars and rogues (or Ben Jonson), moved about on foot.

On some levels of practical experience there were both likenesses and differences between Elizabethan views of nature and ours, and more must be said about differences, even on these levels, as we go on. We may first take a brief look at scientific attitudes. Modern English science began with such notable Elizabethans as Thomas Digges, the chief English Copernican, William Gilbert, Thomas Harriot, William

Harvey, and others. And of course Bacon was inspired by a vision of endless progress through man's conquest of nature; he was at once the prophet of modern science and the last of the universal doctors. From the later Elizabethan age on through what Whitehead called the century of genius, there was a rapid multiplication of scientists, a rapid growth of scientific achievement. But in our period proper, while some laymen like Donne kept up with the new astronomy, literature was affected hardly at all by the new outlook. It was mainly after 1600 that imaginative writers began to allude, uncertainly, to conflicting theories of the celestial system.

One early allusion, a stanza from John Davies' *Orchestra* of 1596, is representative:

> Only the earth doth stand forever still:
> Her rocks remove not, nor her mountains meet,
> Although some wits enriched with learning's skill
> Say heav'n stands firm and that the earth doth fleet,
> And swiftly turneth underneath their feet:
> Yet, though the earth is ever steadfast seen,
> On her broad breast hath dancing ever been.

Thus, half a century after Copernicus, Davies strongly inclines to the traditional geocentric universe, although he respectfully admits the existence of a new and opposed theory. That was more or less the situation of a good many men, then and for some time to come, for a real decision required a mathematical and scientific expertness beyond laymen, who —like us—had to take ideas on trust; and not a few scientists remained sceptical until fuller knowledge and understanding confirmed Copernicus. As a matter of fact, in the years just before and after 1600, there were not two rival theories but three: the geocentric universe of Ptolemy and the Bible and common tradition and common sense; the heliocentric universe of Copernicus; and a compromise developed by the first great modern observer, the Danish Tycho Brahe, who retained the earth as the fixed center but had the five outer planets revolve around the revolving sun. This compromise was for a time attractive to many who could accept neither Ptolemy nor Copernicus. Donne, for instance, seems to have been a Tychonist; and although in his verse and prose he sometimes takes account of new, unsettled, and unsettling knowledge, he normally and instinctively assumes a geocentric world.

In any case, the Copernican doctrine was not nearly so disturbing as modern historians have often said it was. The earth was not dislodged from a supposedly prime place in creation; it had always been considered the basest part. When Thomas Digges speaks of "this little dark star wherein we live," we may think he is going on to a coldly scientific notion of the earth as an insignificant pinpoint; instead, he sees the immensity of the universe as only exalting the glory of its Maker. Unlearned writers like Shakespeare were either unaware of or quite indifferent to the new astronomy. Not to mention many ideas that did not impinge on religion or metaphysics, more serious disturbance could come from other sources than Copernicus. One was the revival of the ancient theory of a plurality of inhabited worlds, which, as Robert Burton noted, raised the problem of such inhabitants' having souls to be saved. Then there were such concrete facts as the appearance of new stars in 1572 and 1604. What made these phenomena upsetting was their contradiction of the age-old belief, supported by both Aristotle and Christian tradition, that the region below the moon, including the earth, was subject to change, but that the heavens above the moon were pure and immutable.

The important thing for writers of the sixteenth century—

and for most of those in the earlier seventeenth also—was that nature was God's creation, that it was man's appointed home and an object to contemplate, not a complex of forces to investigate and exploit. For this religious conception of nature we may go back to the Psalmist's "The heavens declare the glory of God," and his celebrations, in the same spirit, of the beauties and bounties of earth that praise their Creator. For the medieval Catholic Aquinas and the sixteenth-century Protestant Calvin, the book of nature, the book of the creatures, was a revelation of God, secondary, of course, to his Word, but authentic in its degree. The Christian tradition was fortified by the argument from design found in ancient pagan thinkers; a universe of such vastness, such regularity and order, must convince the natural reason that it was framed by a divine mind. In the sixteenth century, and the seventeenth also, scientists as well as laymen shared the religious view. We have observed the attitude of Thomas Digges. How firmly this attitude was established we may judge if we leap up to Newton: although his name is loosely associated with a mechanistic view of the universe, he saw the great system, and all creation, as under God's continuously active care.

We are as much accustomed to the idea of scientific law as to industrial civilization, and it may again require an imaginative effort to see ourselves in what may be called the pre-scientific world of Shakespeare. Perhaps the most eloquent picture of that world is in Hooker:

> And as it cometh to pass in a kingdom rightly ordered, that after a law is once published, it presently takes effect far and wide, all states framing themselves thereunto; even so let us think it fareth in the natural course of the world: since the time that God did first proclaim the edicts of his law upon it, heaven and earth have hearkened unto his voice, and their labour hath been to do his will: He "made

a law for the rain"; He gave his "decree unto the sea, that the waters should not pass his commandment." Now if nature should intermit her course, ànd leave altogether though it were but for a while the observation of her own laws; if those principal and mother elements of the world, whereof all things in this lower world are made, should lose the qualities which now they have; if the frame of that heavenly arch erected over our heads should loosen and dissolve itself; if celestial spheres should forget their wonted motions, and by irregular volubility turn themselves any way as it might happen; if the prince of the lights of heaven, which now as a giant doth run his unwearied course, should as it were through a languishing faintness begin to stand and to rest himself; if the moon should wander from her beaten way, the times and seasons of the year blend themselves by disordered and confused mixture, the winds breathe out their last gasp, the clouds yield no rain, the earth be defeated of heavenly influence, the fruits of the earth pine away as children at the withered breasts of their mother no longer able to yield them relief: what would become of man himself, whom these things now do all serve? See we not plainly that obedience of creatures unto the law of nature is the stay of the whole world?

A word may be added on one special mode of thinking and feeling about the cosmic order which belongs to the tradition of Christian Platonism. *The Governor*, that sober treatise on education for public service by the early Tudor humanist and Platonist, Sir Thomas Elyot, has a large segment on dancing that may puzzle the uninstructed reader—and it may have had many such readers since T. S. Eliot quoted a bit from it in *East Coker*. The theme of Sir Thomas' disquisition is that the regular movements of the dance symbolize all kinds of order, from the courses of the heavenly bodies to matrimony and the moral virtues. Two generations later the young lawyer, John Davies, wrote the poem *Orchestra* which was cited earlier, a graceful Platonic exposition of the cosmic dance of all nature, celestial and terrestrial. And, a couple of generations later still, in *Paradise Lost*, the idea of the starry dance repeatedly kindled Milton's religious imagination into something like mystical fervor.

This whole pre-scientific and religious conception, which links nature closely with God and man, is also a poetic and "mythic" conception. We might consider the rich texture of beliefs and traditions suggested by Marcellus' speech on the platform of Elsinore, after the ghost has vanished:

> It faded on the crowing of the cock.
> Some say that ever, 'gainst that season comes
> Wherein our Saviour's birth is celebrated,
> The bird of dawning singeth all night long;
> And then, they say, no spirit dare stir abroad,
> The nights are wholesome, then no planets strike,
> No fairy takes, nor witch hath power to charm,
> So hallow'd and so gracious is the time.

In the most beautiful of all English love poems, Spenser's *Epithalamion*, marriage is a symbol of religious order, a part of the creative process of a divine world, and all nature shares in the glorious nuptial—the sun, the nymphs of Irish rivers and woods and sea and hills, the warbling birds, the moon and stars. Or we might think of the first movement of Milton's *Nativity* hymn, in which earth and winds and ocean and stars and sun await in hushed expectancy the incarnation of their Maker. God's providential care of nature and man becomes a common theme in the first half of the seventeenth century. For George Herbert man, the child of God, is the center of creation:

> For us the winds do blow,
> The earth doth rest, heav'n move, and fountains flow.
> Nothing we see but means us good.

English Poetry: God and Nature

Andrew Marvell's Puritan exiles, in remote Bermuda, rejoice in God's ever-present care:

> What should we do but sing his praise
> That led us through the wat'ry maze
> Unto an isle so long unknown,
> And yet far kinder than our own?
> Where he the huge sea-monsters wracks,
> That lift the deep upon their backs;
> He lands us on a grassy stage,
> Safe from the storms and prelates' rage.
> He gave us this eternal spring
> Which here enamels everything,
> And sends the fowls to us in care,
> On daily visits through the air.
> He hangs in shades the orange bright,
> Like golden lamps in a green night . . .

Henry Vaughan, the Platonist, sees in all nature the hieroglyphics of divinity, although his vision is not always Platonic. In pure religious tenderness he greets the bird after a stormy night:

> And now as fresh and cheerful as the light,
> Thy little heart in early hymns doth sing
> Unto that Providence whose unseen arm
> Curbed them, and clothed thee well and warm.
>   All things that be praise him, and had
>   Their lesson taught them when first made.

In recalling some of the ways in which man's life was interwoven with nature and God and the supernatural, I have dwelt on the idea of providential order. But the lines quoted from *Hamlet* are a reminder that there was likewise what may almost be called a pattern of natural and supernatural disorder. Shakespeare alone keeps us aware of a multiplicity of violations of order that portend or attend disaster—comets, meteors, and earthquakes, the malign as well as the benign influence of the stars, the activities of ghosts, demons, witches, and so on. And the celebrants of order are not unaware of these things. In Spenser's *Epithalamion* the lover's reverent raptures and his vision of nature's participation carry with them the "feare of perill and foule horror," of lightning, of Puck and "evill sprights," of witches and hobgoblins and damned ghosts, of birds and frogs of ill omen. In Milton's *Nativity*, although Christ is born and false gods are banished, during the long era before the Judgment Satan's energies are only limited, not nullified. On this side of the picture we must be content with two remarks. First, this was not merely a mass of popular superstition. In 1621 the learned Robert Burton, in his "Digression of Divels," provided a wide-ranging catalogue of the maleficent operations of the devil and his agents in nature and in human life; and one could cite other men of learning, including scientists, in England and on the continent, who more or less shared such beliefs. Secondly, these sinister elements of the natural and supernatural, in their impact upon the imagination, are, perhaps more than the doctrine of order, dramatic, poetic, and "mythic" elements in the religious conception of nature.

Even in regard to benign nature I do not mean to say that the Renaissance man or the Renaissance writer had always in his mind the thought of nature as the revelation and the art of God. His senses alone, like ours, might work, as in Spenser's simple and perfect phrase that tells of Sir Calepine's going forth "To take the ayre, and heare the thrushes song," or in Perdita's picture of the daffodils

> That come before the swallow dares and take
> The winds of March with beauty;

or in countless passages of purely sensuous response in these and other Elizabethan poets who, to echo Sidney, made the too much loved earth more lovely. In this connection we might touch on a conspicuous strain in sixteenth-century verse and prose. One of the many classical traditions the Renaissance welcomed was the pastoral, the celebration of an idyllic rural world of happy innocence and youth and beauty and love. This idyllicism was, to be sure, accompanied by a realistic awareness that it was a romantic dream, an escape from the harsh actualities of life, but the pastoral lyric at least could play variations on the dream with a minimum of disenchantment. And to think of famous lyrics, such as Shakespeare's or Marlowe's "Come live with me and be my love," is to remember that the Elizabethan pastoral was not merely a tissue of literary artifice, that classical motifs could be naturalized and fused with homespun song and folklore. We are reminded of that fusion when Orsino, in *Twelfth Night*, calls for a certain old, plain song:

> The spinsters and the knitters in the sun,
> And the free maids that weave their thread with bones,
> Do use to chant it. It is silly sooth,
> And dallies with the innocence of love,
> Like the old age.

But if the common responses to nature, whether direct or in the idealizing pastoral vein, were simple and sensuous, it was still of the first importance that the religious and mythic conception was in the background. It could, when assumed, add an aura to mere description, or it could be fully developed, as in Milton's account of Creation in the seventh book of *Paradise Lost*, an account bursting with the dynamic and divine idea of birth and growth and movement. This passage, moreover, is a massive reminder of a fundamental point: that Milton and many other poets did not feel that division between the One and the Many that has so often tormented artists and thinkers. Whatever the strength of evil, all nature and all truth were linked together by analogy and correspondence in a grand unity.

This total conception of nature remained both possible and instinctive through a good part of the seventeenth century, until scientific rationalism ate away the links of the great chain of being and even, for some minds, the throne from which the chain descended. Good liberals may see nothing but good in such enlightenment. Yet, when we move up to the time of modern scientific analysis and exploitation (however inevitable and necessary these advances were), we may arrive at John Dewey's sobering reflection that nature, in ceasing to be divine, has ceased to be human. We have witnessed in some modern poets, such as Yeats, the effort to find an imaginative substitute for the supernatural world of an earlier day.

IV

English Poetry: Time and Man

GOD, NATURE, AND MAN are obvious and foreordained headings for any consideration of the human outlook on life, but the heading "Time" may at first thought seem a dubious interloper. However, a second thought—if a second be needed—recalls the peculiarly insistent and poignant consciousness of devouring Time that inspires much of the finest writing of our period. It is so fine indeed that I do not apologize for letting this part of my discourse turn into a small anthology; one is inclined rather to apologize for letting blocks of comment dull the golden mosaic of poetry. But before we come to illustrations we may remind ourselves of two or three definable differences between our and the Renaissance view of time. (By "our" I do not mean the metaphysical-mathematical conceptions of modern thinkers, which I could not venture to approach, but only the ordinary notions with which we live.)

Renaissance minds—and ancient minds too—conceived of infinite space, even if their idea of infinity fell far short of space measured in light-years; but the idea of time was much more limited. Even in the nineteenth century educated people could still think of the Creation as having occurred in 4004 B.C. (the date set by seventeenth-century chronologers, some of whom could name the day and the hour). For us the origins of the earth and the universe have been pushed so far back that informed guesses can differ by millions of years, and the future seems to provide small ground for guessing at all. The modern mind, whether religious or non-religious, is aware, or half-aware, of time as an endless continuum, in which the span of recorded history is a very tiny segment. With that vast, vague conception of time our emotions are not much involved; they are involved—like the emotions of all men of all ages—with the duration of our own lives and the lives of those about us.

For thoughtful men of the Renaissance such universal private feelings were conditioned, and sometimes greatly heightened, both by the general conception of time and by several more or less traditional beliefs that could go along with that. First and most obviously, time was rather a religious than a scientific idea. World history was pivoted on three supreme events: the Creation and the life and death of Christ, the first as well as the second within a measurable past, and, in the not immeasurably remote future, the end of the world and the day of judgment. Secondly, according to a tradition we meet especially in the earlier seventeenth century, the history of man on earth was divided into three equal periods: the 2000 years from the Creation to Moses, the 2000 years of the Mosaic law, up to the birth of Christ, and 2000 of the Christian dispensation. The most famous statement of this threefold division is in one of Donne's sermons, where he is using it incidentally in an effort to make conceivable the idea of eternity:

> A day that hath no *pridie*, nor *postridie;* yesterday doth not usher it in, nor to-morrow shall not drive it out. Methusalem, with all his hundreds of years, was but a mushroom of a night's growth, to this day. And all the four monarchies, with all their thousands of years, and all the powerful kings, and all the beautiful queens of this world, were but as a bed of flowers, some gathered at six, some at seven, some at eight, all in one morning, in respect of this day. In all the two thousand years of nature, before the law given by Moses, and the two thousand years of law, before the gospel given by Christ, and the two thousand of grace, which are running now (of which last hour we have heard three quarters strike, more than fifteen hundred of this last two thousand spent), in all this six thousand, and in all those which God may be pleased to add, *in domo patris,* in this house of his Father's, there was never heard quarter clock to strike, never seen minute glass to turn.

Thus Donne, speaking in 1626, thinks of more than three-fourths of the last period of the world as having run out. And a generation later Sir Thomas Browne, in the century's grandest descant on the theme, sees men of his age as born "in this setting part of time," when it is too late to be ambitious.

With this religious belief in a limited future could be associated the more scientific belief that all the energies of nature, in and outside man, were flagging, sinking toward the ultimate dissolution. Spenser, in the proem to Book V of *The Faerie Queene*, sets forth the idea of decline from the golden age, and uses a scientific argument—the altered position of the sun since Ptolemy's time—that continued to figure in discussion. For in the later sixteenth and the early seventeenth century there was voluminous and earnest debate on this question, the optimistic progressives opposing the pessimistic deteriorationists. To mention only two famous names on the edge of the debate, Ben Jonson and the young Milton both vigorously rejected the doctrine of nature's decay.

Along with these religio-scientific beliefs or ideas, which affected some men, there were concrete evidences of the workings of time and mutability that no one could miss. In an age of intrigue, violence, and almost absolute royal authority, the wheel of fortune might elevate or destroy with equal suddenness. The fall of great men from high estate filled the dolorous pages of the *Mirror for Magistrates*, which contributed something to the growth of Elizabethan tragedy. The Wars of the Roses, in histories and in Shakespeare's and other plays, were a long story of conflicting ambitions, broken allegiance, crimes, cruelties, the block, and the battlefield. The changes in religion under the Tudors sent many people into exile, some to the scaffold, and, especially in the grim reign of Mary, many to the stake. But one does not need to multiply such reminders of the "tickle, trustless" state of man. Nor does one need to rehearse, in prose, the feelings that people in all ages have in regard to youth and love and age and death, the whole pageant of passing time. Even such ravages of "Time's fell hand" as the decay of ancient towns and buildings inspired meditations that ranged from Spenser's "antiquarian" poems (based partly on Du Bellay) to Shakespeare's sonnets. And to think of these last is to remember many other aspects of time, from autumnal decay—"Bare ruin'd choirs where late the sweet birds sang"—to the proud declaration that

Not marble nor the gilded monuments
Of princes shall outlive this pow'rful rhyme.

The examples that we can recall are familiar, but no repetition can dull the high tension and intensity that Renaissance writers brought to the contemplation of time. While these examples cannot be neatly classified, we might try to follow three main themes, love, death, and mutability; and we may observe the presence, sometimes in the same man, of Christian and pagan attitudes, religious faith and the pride of life contending against each other.

The traditional attitude toward love crystallized in Horace's phrase *carpe diem* is of course pagan in its essence, and that pagan note was struck in thousands of Renaissance poems, in Latin and in the vernaculars. One of the simplest English versions is Shakespeare's lyric, "O mistress mine," which is in the form and style of popular song but develops the classical text:

> What is love? 'Tis not hereafter;
> Present mirth hath present laughter;
>   What's to come is still unsure:
> In delay there lies no plenty;
> Then come kiss me, sweet and twenty!
>   Youth's a stuff will not endure.

For a direct and sober classical echo there is Campion's paraphrase of Catullus:

> My sweetest Lesbia, let us live and love,
> And though the sager sort our deeds reprove,
> Let us not weigh them. Heav'n's great lamps do dive
> Into their west, and straight again revive,
> But soon as once set is our little light,
> Then must we sleep one ever-during night.

Ben Jonson's version of Catullus, "Come, my Celia, let us prove," takes a lighter view of love and time, in keeping with its dramatic context. *Corinna's Going A-Maying*, by the chief of the "sons of Ben," is in the classical tradition, although it is an original, graceful, and subtle interweaving of nature and

man, the pagan and the Christian, and although its theme is
not merely young love but the brevity of all life. It is in the
sombre conclusion that the classical note is heard, the note
heard so often from this Anglican clergyman:

> Come, let us go while we are in our prime,
> And take the harmless folly of the time.
>   We shall grow old apace, and die
>   Before we know our liberty.
>   Our life is short, and our days run
>   As fast away as does the sun;
> And as a vapor, or a drop of rain
> Once lost, can ne'er be found again,
>   So when or you or I are made
>   A fable, song, or fleeting shade,
>   All love, all liking, all delight
>   Lies drowned with us in endless night.
> Then while time serves, and we are but decaying,
> Come, my Corinna, come, let's go a-Maying.

The finest and most familiar poem in the tradition of *carpe
diem*, *To his Coy Mistress*, is classical in its symmetry, clarity,
and elegance and in the direct exhortation of the final paragraph. Although that paragraph is complex too, Marvell is
more fully "metaphysical" and original in the playful wit of
the opening theme, "Had we but world enough, and time,"
and in the sudden change to realistic and reverberating
ironies:

> But at my back I always hear
> Time's wingèd chariot hurrying near;
> And yonder all before us lie
> Deserts of vast eternity . . . .

While love poems on the theme of *carpe diem* generally
bear some marks of the classical tradition, no recognizable

convention affects the manner and tone of those poems which
proclaim a love that is impervious to time and may survive life
itself. Lord Herbert, in his pastoral-philosophical *Ode, upon
a Question Moved, Whether Love Should Continue Forever?*,
answers yes: love in the soul must outlive the death of the
body. In Shakespeare's sonnets, as I remarked earlier, the
thought of time broods darkly over all experience; he rings
the changes on the brevity of life and beauty, the insecurity
of friendship and love and faith and hope. Yet one of the
greatest sonnets is an impassioned defiance of time:

> Love's not Time's fool, though rosy lips and cheeks
> Within his bending sickle's compass come.
> Love alters not with his brief hours and weeks,
> But bears it out even to the edge of doom.

The first two lines, by the way, with their common personifi-
cation of Chronos (Time) or Saturn, illustrate the fashion, so
instinctive with Renaissance poets, in which an abstract idea
becomes concrete and "mythic."

Apart from the legion of Petrarchan sonneteers, whose
protestations seldom move us, the most fervent asserter of
enduring love was Donne. In his more irresponsible pieces
Donne can glorify inconstancy and promiscuity, but in more
sober moods, especially in poems that may have been ad-
dressed to his wife, he inhabits another world, the world of
love that he himself builds up in opposition to the world of
everyday affairs. That busy old fool, the unruly sun, may call
the rest of mankind to daily work, but

> Love, all alike, no season knows, nor clime,
> Nor hours, days, months, which are the rags of time.

If travel and separation from his beloved should end in his
death, let her

> But think that we
> Are but turned aside to sleep;
> They who one another keep
> Alive, ne'er parted be.

Donne's grand affirmation in this vein is *The Anniversary:*

> All kings, and all their favorites,
> All glory of honors, beauties, wits,
> The sun itself, which makes times as they pass,
> Is elder by a year now than it was
> When thou and I first one another saw;
> All other things to their destruction draw,
> Only our love hath no decay;
> This no to-morrow hath, nor yesterday,
> Running, it never runs from us away,
> But truly keeps his first, last, everlasting day.

Whether or not these last lines carry love beyond death, we may note that one of them anticipates a phrase in Donne's later picture of eternity that was quoted before—"A day that hath no *pridie,* nor *postridie;* yesterday doth not usher it in, nor to-morrow shall not drive it out." Certainly in *The Canonization* love survives death. From the explosive repudiation of the everyday world of careerists, Donne moves to a quiet conclusion where, in religious terms, he creates a world of love in which the two ideal lovers have become saints, to be invoked by lovers still on earth.

Other themes than love link time with death, and death, like time, was half-personified. The medieval and pictorial tradition of the Dance of Death remained vivid in the imagination of later ages. From Chaucer's *Pardoner's Tale*, or the *Ludus Coventriae* play in which Death glides into Herod's banquet hall and surveys his victims, we move up through the centuries to, say, the image of Death the Leveler in James Shirley's lyric:

> The glories of our blood and state
>> Are shadows, not substantial things,
> There is no armor against fate;
>> Death lays his icy hand on kings;

or to *Paradise Lost* and the biblical allegory of the foul figures of Sin and Death following Satan to earth to prey henceforth upon mankind.

One sort of reaction in this period, which we may call pagan, is the view of death as simply the end of life, the complete extinction of a vital personality—in the words of Claudio, in *Measure for Measure*,

> Ay, but to die, and go we know not where;
> To lie in cold obstruction and to rot;
> This sensible warm motion to become
> A kneaded clod . . . .

To call this pagan is not to say that a given speaker was non-Christian—Claudio goes on to imagine hell—but only that a particular utterance might stress negation or annihilation. Thus the young Chidiock Tichborne, about to be executed for complicity in a Catholic plot against Elizabeth, was the author, or the subject, of verses that have a refrain of stark finality: "And now I live, and now my life is done." Whatever degree of Christian atmosphere we allow or do not allow to *Hamlet*, the hero's reflections in the graveyard are almost purely pagan: the skulls of the politician, the courtier, the lawyer whose documents will not help him now, and of Yorick, the king's jester, whose flashes of merriment were wont to set the table on a roar; and the fine lady whose paint is an inch thick must come to this same state, for even the noble dust of Alexander may serve to stop a bunghole. The dirge in *Cymbeline*, although concerned with early death, has a partly parallel theme:

Fear no more the heat o' th' sun,
   Nor the furious winter's rages;
Thou thy worldly task hast done,
   Home art gone, and ta'en thy wages.
Golden lads and girls all must,
As chimney-sweepers, come to dust.

The magical and mythical dirge of Ariel, "Full fathom five thy father lies," is outside all categories; and, in this last of Shakespeare's "miracle plays," we have Prospero's brief summary of the human condition:

                    We are such stuff
As dreams are made on, and our little life
Is rounded with a sleep.

There are many things and many writers—notably Webster, who "was much possessed by death"—one would like to recall, but these "pagan" examples may end with that apostrophe in Ralegh's *History of the World* in which Death appears as the silent agent of divine justice more fearfully effective upon the heart of man than all God's words:

> O eloquent, just, and mighty Death! whom none could advise, thou hast persuaded; what none hath dared, thou hast done; and whom all the world hath flattered, thou only hast cast out of the world and despised; thou hast drawn together all the far-stretched greatness, all the pride, cruelty, and ambition of man, and covered it all over with these two narrow words, *Hic iacet*.

When we turn to positively religious reactions to death, we think at once of Dr. Faustus, whose last speech was partly quoted before. Faustus' agonized fear of death and damnation is bound up with his desperate awareness of time moving swiftly to the appointed hour, an awareness doubly terrible

74

for one who, at the height of his delusive *hubris*, had called upon the phantom of Helen of Troy to make him immortal with a kiss. That potent symbol of youth and beauty and love works its full effect in the famous stanza of Thomas Nashe:

> Beauty is but a flower
> Which wrinkles will devour;
> Brightness falls from the air,
> Queens have died young and fair,
> Dust hath closed Helen's eye.
> I am sick, I must die.
>   Lord, have mercy on us!

The body of the stanza might be called pagan, although it is in the medieval tradition of *Ubi sunt* that we associate especially with Villon, but the refrain is a Christian prayer in a time of plague. As a pendant to Ralegh's apostrophe, we might recall those no less familiar lines of his which originally concluded an amatory pagan poem but were apparently rewritten just before his execution. In this last solemn and sombre testament he looks beyond mortality:

> Even such is Time, which takes in trust
> Our youth, our joys, and all we have,
> And pays us but with age and dust;
> Who in the dark and silent grave,
> When we have wandered all our ways,
> Shuts up the story of our days:
> And from which earth and grave and dust,
> The Lord shall raise me up, I trust.

On this theme Donne alone would provide an anthology of verse and prose, from the sonnet "Death, be not proud," in which the poet challenges the great enemy in the strength of Christian faith, up to his last sermon, "Death's Duel." And the sermon reminds us of Walton's account of the preacher's elaborate preparations for his own death, a ceremonial at once religious, theatrical, and macabre. Since we glanced at *Corinna's Going A-Maying*, we might remember that, as religious poet, Herrick prayerfully anticipates wearing a golden coronet in heaven.

In speaking of nature I touched on pastoral idyllicism, and here I might touch on the pastoral elegy. Whereas the classical elegy was likely to stress the eternal sleep of death, in the Christian tradition, exemplified in Spenser's *November* eclogue and supremely in *Lycidas*, the conclusion becomes a triumphant affirmation of immortality—and, for Milton, a triumphant answer to his questioning of God's justice:

> Weep no more, woeful shepherds, weep no more,
> For Lycidas, your sorrow, is not dead,
> Sunk though he be beneath the wat'ry floor;
> So sinks the day-star in the ocean bed,
> And yet anon repairs his drooping head,
> And tricks his beams, and with new-spangled ore
> Flames in the forehead of the morning sky:
> So Lycidas sunk low, but mounted high,
> Through the dear might of him that walked the waves,
> Where, other groves and other streams along,
> With nectar pure his oozy locks he laves,
> And hears the unexpressive nuptial song
> In the blest kingdoms meek of joy and love.
> There entertain him all the saints above,
> In solemn troops and sweet societies
> That sing, and singing in their glory move,
> And wipe the tears for ever from his eyes.

I cannot leave the theme of death without mentioning one great elegy that does not belong to the pastoral genre, Henry King's *Exequy* on his young wife. The whole poem is a series of variations on the idea of time, above all the slow passage of days and years that delay his reunion with her:

'Tis true, with shame and grief I yield,
Thou like the van first tookst the field,
And gotten hath the victory
In thus adventuring to die
Before me, whose more years might crave
A just precedence in the grave.
But hark! my pulse like a soft drum
Beats my approach, tells thee I come;
And slow howe'er my marches be,
I shall at last sit down by thee.

Our third heading, mutability, has had much illustration
already, but I should like to link together two large works
which are notable in themselves and notably characteristic of
their authors. These are Spenser's *Two Cantos of Mutability*,
which were written in the late 1590's and published as a fragment after his death, and Donne's *Anniversaries*, which were
written and published in 1611–12. Spenser's *Cantos*, although
a fragment, constitute a complete unit. The vehicle is an original myth that starts from the ancient myth of the war of the
gods and Titans. The Titaness Mutability claims the sovereignty of the world and challenges the power of Jove and the
other Olympians. Her case is heard before the supreme deity,
Nature, whose sergeant, we may observe, is Order. In support
of her claim Mutability displays a pageant of the changing
seasons, months, hours, day and night and life and death.
Nature's verdict is the verdict of orthodox Christian tradition,
that continual change is a fact, but that it is not mere chance
and accident; it is part of an evolutionary process under the
control of God's providence. But what adds another dimen-
sion to the poem, and brings us close to the heart of the poet,
is the two stanzas that seem to be forced from him when he
meditates on Nature's judgment. The devoutly Christian poet
accepts that judgment, yet he is so overwhelmed by his sense
of the immediate sway of Mutability on earth that he utters

an anguished cry of longing for the peace and stability of
heaven:

When I bethinke me on that speech whyleare,
  Of Mutability, and well it way:
  Me seemes, that though she all unworthy were
  Of the Heav'ns Rule; yet very sooth to say,
  In all things else she beares the greatest sway.
  Which makes me loath this state of life so tickle,
  And love of things so vaine to cast away;
  Whose flowring pride, so fading and so fickle,
Short Time shall soon cut down with his consuming
    sickle.

Then gin I thinke on that which Nature sayd,
  Of that same time when no more Change shall be,
  But stedfast rest of all things firmely stayd
  Upon the pillours of Eternity,
  That is contrayr to Mutabilitie:
  For, all that moveth, doth in Change delight:
  But thence-forth all shall rest eternally
  With Him that is the God of Sabbaoth hight:
O! that great Sabbaoth God, grant me that Sabaoths
    sight.

Much has been written about Donne's *Anniversaries* in the
last thirty years, but all that must be taken for granted in these
few remarks. The two poems, as everyone knows, are osten-
sibly elegies on the young Elizabeth Drury, although her
death is only a symbol of the order and perfection that man
has lost. The poems are organized, as Louis L. Martz has
shown, in the manner of traditional exercises in meditation,
and their "metaphysical" texture is as far as it could be from
that of Spenser's epic myth. And whereas Spenser was largely
pre-scientific in his outlook, the younger Donne had an up-to-
date knowledge of the new science and could add its vain-

glorious results to his other evidence of man's prideful effort to gloss over his corruption. But the reactions of the sophisticated Donne are not so far from Spenser's as we might expect. Spenser's theme, to be sure, is mutability, and Donne's—although he takes in the world's change and decay—is the sinfulness of man and the way of purgation and conversion; yet both as a matter of course look beyond earthly life and darkness to the goal and the light of heaven. Both, in the spirit of *contemptus mundi*, call in the next world to redress the balance of this.

If an active consciousness of heaven (and hell) were still a general possession, it would be superfluous to demonstrate that Christian poets were Christian poets. But we might call a few more witnesses who appealed to the same final resource, in simply religious or half-Platonic terms. We think of Sir Philip Sidney, the English model of the Renaissance man:

> Leave me, O love which reachest but to dust;
> And thou, my mind, aspire to higher things;
> Grow rich in that which never taketh rust,
> Whatever fades but fading pleasure brings . . .
>
> Then farewell, world; thy uttermost I see;
> Eternal Love, maintain thy life in me.

The young John Milton, as yet an untried idealist, could contemplate the divine order with single-hearted fervor (as indeed he always did). In the *Nativity*, glancing back at the Creation and forward to the Last Judgment, he celebrated the Incarnation as the beginning of a new harmony between heaven and earth. In the poems *On Time* and *At a Solemn Music*, and in *Comus*, he turned away, in the spirit of Christian Platonism, from the gross vanities and jarring discords of earthly life to the pure and harmonious order of eternity.

About the same time George Herbert, cataloguing the sweet things of earth that must quickly die, could affirm, in a metaphysical image of quiet sublimity:

Only a sweet and virtuous soul,
Like seasoned timber, never gives;
But though the whole world turn to coal,
    Then chiefly lives.

A quarter of a century later Sir Thomas Browne dwells on the vanity of pagan satisfaction in earthly monuments: "But all this is nothing in the metaphysics of true belief," for the Christian is "ready to be anything, in the ecstasy of being ever."

Our last large heading is man, and our time for considering him may seem even more inadequate than it is. But of course everything that has been said already, about God, nature, and time, bears directly on the spiritual constitution and situation of man. Writers of the Renaissance could, like most modern writers, deal with man in wholly or mainly naturalistic terms, yet even such treatments could hardly avoid the higher and deeper dimensions and reverberations that go with a religious view of the world and human destiny. That man was made in the image of God, that he stands midway between the angels and the beasts and is pulled in both directions by his dual nature, that his life on earth is a brief prelude to an eternity of bliss or torment, that he perpetuates the sin of Adam, that his salvation was made possible by the suffering of the Redeemer and the continued efficacy of grace, that he is God's chief earthly creature, the center and lord of the visible world, that he is the microcosmic parallel to the macrocosm, that his soul is a similar scene of conflict between good and evil—all these and other articles of faith are in either the foreground or the background of literature. It is clear that the stage of human action is infinitely larger, that the consequences of action are of infinitely greater import, than they can be when the common conception of man is bounded by the data of biology, psychology, and such ethical standards as are implied in the magic word "adjustment." With this last, to be sure, writers of our age are not concerned; and the Renaissance Christian-classical belief in man's fall from primal perfection has had a kind of resurgence in the theme of guilt that appears in much modern writing.

Before touching on some ways in which these beliefs operated, we may remember that the Renaissance writer inherited, and held with fervor, the classical doctrine that literature is delightful teaching. To be sure, there are poems that are works of pure art, and comedy that is pure (and often earthy) entertainment; but the general theory of literature was didactic. One concrete and conspicuous part of this theory, amply illustrated in Sidney's *Defence of Poesy*, was belief in the potency of examples, examples of virtue to be emulated, of wickedness to be abhorred. Such principles may be thought naïve, but the products of the ethical imagination commonly transcended naïveté.

One such product was Sidney's own romance in prose, the *Arcadia*, which was really a "heroical poem," but we may look at a still more comprehensive and more familiar work, *The Faerie Queene*. We remember the author's aim, to fashion a gentleman or noble person in virtuous and gentle discipline, and we remember also his ethical reading of ancient and modern heroic poems in the light of which he wrote his own. In each book Spenser sets up the ideal or norm of the chosen virtue and shows in action both approximations to the ideal and a wide array of departures from it. Such a bald description of the ethical skeleton does not of course begin to explain the power and beauty and subtlety of the poem. One element in Spenser's conception must be mentioned. He treats such classical and Renaissance virtues as Temperance, Chastity, Friendship, Justice, and Courtesy, but the first book deals with the very un-Aristotelian virtue of Holiness. Here that common figure of medieval romance, the unpromising hero, is transmuted into the untried Christian soldier, who arrives at holiness only through experience of sin and despair, and with the aid of Truth and Grace personified in Una and Arthur. The second book takes up the classical virtue of Temperance, and its hero is a man equipped with reason, the power of moral choice. Yet it is in this book only that a protecting angel appears, and the exhausted hero is further protected by Arthur. In saving Guyon, Arthur now represents—to follow A. S. P. Woodhouse's interpretation—not the grace that works upon the inward man, but the intervention of Providence in the natural world. Moreover, this second book has two endings. The rational Guyon accomplishes his quest by destroying the Bower of Bliss, the home of sensuality. But it is left to Arthur to defend the house of Alma, the Soul, against Maleger and his band. If Woodhouse is right in his brilliant suggestion that Maleger represents original sin, it is significant that it is only Arthur, and not Guyon, who can defeat him. Thus, Spenser seems to say (in more than one place), reason is the helpmate of virtue, but it has not by itself sufficient strength to kill the inveterate root of sin.

As a good Anglican, Spenser was a good Calvinist, yet even this glance at *The Faerie Queene* indicates the general fact that so-called Calvinistic determinism did not absolve man from his prime moral responsibility, as in theory we might expect. Such individual responsibility is found everywhere in Renaissance literature; psychological and social enlightenment was much too elementary to exonerate the criminal and transfer the blame to society. As Pico della Mirandola had said long before, in his famous discourse on human dignity, God gave man the capacity to sink to the level of the brute or to mount to the divine, according to the sentence of his intellect. The problem was whether the will would actively support the moral reason's insight. Montaigne arrived at an easy-going naturalism that was neither gross nor heroic, and was happy to accept himself as he was; he had neither an angel's conscience nor a horse's conscience but a man's conscience. And many men, in life and in literature, moved on that level, or below it. But more exalted and exacting spirits could not be thus satisfied; they felt the demands of a higher ideal. Moreover, as Renaissance thought came to maturity, the old clearcut antitheses were complicated by questioning: what was the basis for traditional moral assumptions, for the traditional "knowledge" of man? To practical and universal moral problems was added the conscious scrutiny of the problem of knowledge and authority.

As we observed earlier, the Elizabethans, along with orthodox Christian faith, accepted in more or less sophisticated ways the rational and moral absolutes that Christianity had assimilated from classical thought. As we also observed, Renaissance scepticism, likewise a classical inheritance, had by 1600 made large headway on the continent but not much in England. Yet some questioning of tradition was in the air, and it was stimulated by such diverse forces as the Reformation and the growth of experimental science. "What do I know?" was Montaigne's great question, and English writers, much less sceptical than Montaigne, were beginning to feel the same kind of pressure, to be on the defensive. Bacon, combining religious sincerity and highmindedness with a scientific bias, could separate the realm of knowledge, the nature open to scientific inquiry, from the realm of faith; and such a separation, however necessary, was in the end to make a deep fissure in what had been accepted as the divine unity of all creation. Further, Bacon could apply the empirical method to practical ethics and approve of Machiavelli's concern with what men do and not with what they ought to do. But traditional morality, from the ancients down, had been concerned with what men ought to do. And, as I have been saying, the central tradition of Christian humanism assumed moral absolutes that the right reason of man could and must comprehend: were not Adam and Eve the types of human pride, seeking knowledge and finding corruption? How far should inquiry go?

We have already met the young lawyer, John Davies, as the author of a serene Platonic poem on the dance as the symbol of cosmic order. His later and less serene poem, *Nosce Teipsum*, begins with the problem of knowledge. To quote some stanzas on Adam and Eve:

> Even so by tasting of that fruit forbid,
>   Where they sought knowledge, they did error find;
>   Ill they desired to know, and ill they did,
>   And to give passion eyes, made reason blind.
>
> For then their minds did first in passion see
>   Those wretched shapes of misery and woe,
>   Of nakedness, of shame, of poverty,
>   Which then their own experience made them know.
>
> But then grew reason dark, that she no more
>   Could the fair forms of good and truth discern;
>   Bats they became, that eagles were before,
>   And this they got by their desire to learn.
>
> But we, their wretched offspring, what do we?
>   Do not we still taste of the fruit forbid,
>   Whiles with fond fruitless curiosity
>   In books profane we seek for knowledge hid?

Samuel Daniel was perhaps less troubled than Davies and

others because he had stronger confidence in the power of culture. When he saluted knowledge as "Soul of the world," he meant, not science, but the humanities, wisdom. In his weighty ethical epistles he celebrates those happy men who have risen above the passions and turmoil of perplexed and distressed humanity. And he sets up, as a humane ideal, a saying of Seneca which Montaigne had put beyond the reach of the natural man:

> And that unless above himself he can
> Erect himself, how poor a thing is man!

Toward the achievement of such high stability, literature, culture, is the great aid; it sustains judgment and conscience against mere "opinion."

Two more tough-minded and more difficult poets, George Chapman and Fulke Greville, had much to say on this problem of knowledge. *The Tears of Peace* is Chapman's chief direct statement of his earnest humanistic and religious gospel. Mere learning makes man only a walking dictionary. True learning is wisdom that nourishes the soul, God's image sent from heaven, and enables it to rule the body's mutinous realm. Chapman carried his creed not only into his tragedies, as Ennis Rees has admirably shown, but even into the translation of the Homer whom he revered as the supreme poet and teacher. In his preface to the *Odyssey* he draws an eloquent contrast between Achilles and his ideal hero, Odysseus:

> In one, predominant perturbation; in the other, overruling wisdom: in one, the body's fervor and fashion of outward fortitude to all possible height of heroical action; in the other, the mind's inward, constant, and unconquered empire, unbroken, unaltered, with any most insolent and tyrannous infliction.

85

George Lord has expounded Chapman's interpretation of the *Odyssey* as the depiction of a man's moral growth from rashness to wisdom.

Fulke Greville, a man of the world and a statesman as well as a poet, had something less than Chapman's positive faith in man's potentialities, and his pessimism was intensified by his Calvinistic sense of human depravity. Most fully in his *Treaty of Human Learning*, Greville gives a dark picture of intellectual and moral disorder. Man's accumulated knowledge has left him in almost hopeless confusion. Greville can only plead that knowledge be sifted, purified, and made fruitful.

The most familiar utterances on this theme are two passages in Donne. The lines beginning "And new philosophy calls all in doubt," in the first *Anniversary*, have been quoted a thousand times in recent decades and need not be quoted here. The passage on man's ignorance in the second *Anniversary* (lines 261 f.) is less threadbare. With all the progress of science, Donne says, we do not know what elements the body is made of, or how the blood circulates (this was four years before Harvey spoke), or why blood is red and grass is green. His answer is not that of Daniel or Chapman or Greville; still less—in spite of Donne's knowledge of science—is it that of the modernist Bacon. Donne dismisses science, the reports of the senses, as pedantry; the only true knowledge will be revealed in heaven. There—or through religious humility on earth—

> Thou shalt not peep through lattices of eyes,
> Nor hear through labyrinths of ears, nor learn
> By circuit or collections to discern.

In the *Anatomy of Melancholy* the omniscient Robert Burton, after surveying the bewildering confusion of astronomical theories, seeks refuge in the same answer. To leap up for a moment to *Paradise Lost,* the dialogue on astronomy takes that kind of knowledge as useless for man's essential life, and the dangers of such irreligious pride are set forth at large in the temptation and fall of Eve.

This fear of excessive "curiosity," the demand for temperance in knowledge, may be condemned at once as mere obscurantism, but that would be a shallow verdict. These writers are not damning all secular knowledge in itself; they are insisting on a hierarchy of values, and their position has often been reaffirmed in our age of atomic and hydrogen bombs. The heart of man, as Daniel said, is "the centre of this world." And Milton's Adam, after the fall, is given the hope of "a paradise within thee, happier far" than Eden. But frail man, the chief of creatures, living in the temporal and animal world yet linked with the eternal, can hardly hope to achieve inward order and unity. The poignant sense of the contrast between what he is and what he would be, of his inhabiting a plane between the superhuman and the subhuman, runs through writing of all kinds (and the contrast has of course its comic side too). When Faustus has been carried away by the devils, the chorus laments:

> Cut is the branch that might have grown full straight,
> And burned is Apollo's laurel bough,
> That sometime grew within this learned man;

and it goes on to condemn the practice of "more than heavenly power permits." Two witnesses may be quoted again. This is John Davies:

> I know my life's a pain and but a span,
>   I know my sense is mocked with everything;
>   And to conclude, I know myself a man,
>   Which is a proud and yet a wretched thing.

Fulke Greville provides one of the most direct and moving statements:

> Oh, wearisome condition of humanity,
> Born under one law, to another bound;
> Vainly begot, and yet forbidden vanity;
> Created sick, commanded to be sound.
> What meaneth nature by these diverse laws?
> Passion and reason self-division cause.

Doubtless the most familiar variations on man's dual status are those of Hamlet (I follow the punctuation of the second Quarto):

> What piece of work is a man, how noble in reason, how infinite in faculties, in form, and moving, how express and admirable in action, how like an angel in apprehension, how like a god: the beauty of the world; the paragon of animals; and yet to me, what is this quintessence of dust?

One may add Hamlet's brief question, "What should such fellows as I do, crawling between earth and heaven?" In the opening speech of the Soul in Marvell's *Dialogue between the Soul and the Body* we have paradoxes akin to those in the lines from Donne's second *Anniversary:*

> Oh, who shall from this dungeon raise
> A soul enslaved so many ways?
> With bolts of bones; that fettered stands
> In feet, and manacled in hands;
> Here blinded with an eye, and there
> Deaf with the drumming of an ear;
> A soul hung up, as 'twere, in chains
> Of nerves and arteries and veins;
> Tortured, besides each other part,
> In a vain head and double heart.

And there are the changes rung, with less agitation, by that metaphysical poet of prose, Sir Thomas Browne:

> But man is a noble animal, splendid in ashes, and pompous in the grave, solemnizing nativities and deaths with equal lustre, nor omitting ceremonies of bravery in the infamy of his nature.

Thus the troubled, even despairing, sense of man's inescapable duality, of his being pulled at once toward the bestial and the angelic, bound up individual moral struggles, defeats, and victories with the divine order of the world and supplied the conditions for tragedy of more than human and temporal import. Is not this conception of man one chief cause of the unique greatness of utterance in this period, a conception that embraced lower depths and loftier heights and richer tensions than are comprehended in the naturalistic view? And while we live in another world, we can return to these old and great writers and breathe at times a finer air than our own.

This survey has been not only sketchy but lopsided, in drawing its illustrations mainly from non-dramatic poets. But it is those writers who express ideas most directly, whereas Shakespeare and other dramatists of course deal more or less impersonally with individual characters in particular situations, so that these dramatists' personal beliefs and attitudes are matters of sometimes elusive inference. Although we cannot at this stage survey Elizabethan and Jacobean drama, one question may be broached. It has been said that any theological suggestion of a compensating heaven is fatal to tragedy, although one remembers that it is not fatal to *Hamlet*—"And flights of angels sing thee to thy rest!" Certainly the Elizabethan and Jacobean age was the great age of English tragic writing, and, as we have been reminding ourselves, the general temper and the writers of this age were more or less positively Christian; unless the dramatists were a race apart, there would seem to be a contradiction somewhere. Shakespeare, to be sure, may be said to remain a great enigma, notwithstanding some modern efforts to make him a poet of Christian symbolism. It can be, and has been, shown that he is full of references to the common body of beliefs and assumptions that we have been reviewing, and that, so far as his own attitude can be divined, it often appears to be in accord with that of other men, from the central articles of Christian faith to ideals of political and cosmic order. Yet how far, in Shakespeare's deepest soundings of good and evil in human nature and experience, he may have moved beyond those orthodox ways of thought and feeling, that is the question. If, for example, there are clear Christian overtones in *Hamlet* and *King Lear*, are these only overtones or are they something more? And do Christian premises underlie, say, the exaltation and the ruin of Antony and Cleopatra? But Shakespeare is not to be crowded into a last paragraph. As Spenser, shrinking from the attempt to describe the goddess Nature, referred the reader to Geoffrey Chaucer and Alanus de Insulis, perhaps I may refer to a book by Geoffrey Bush, *Shakespeare and the Natural Condition*, a book which, to speak with paternal objectivity, has some wise things to say on these great questions.

V

The Isolation of the
Renaissance Hero

ONE OF THE CLICHÉS of our time is that the common isolation
of the romantic and the modern hero reflects the sense of
alienation from society felt by many romantic and modern
artists and intellectuals. (It might be remarked, by the way,
that such aliens appear to be in danger of losing their special
standing, since society itself is now seen as the lonely crowd.)
This is of course a stereotype of the past century and a half,
not the norm of cultural history. It would be hard to think of
any ancients who felt isolated in the modern sense; even Socrates saw himself as a citizen of Athens. And we might try to
imagine the result of putting the question "Do you feel isolated?" to Chaucer or Rabelais or Shakespeare or Cervantes
(although Don Quixote is the supreme example of romantic
isolation, seen in a comic light). If the romantic or modern
hero is usually isolated because of rebellious nonconformity
or the recoil of a superior nature from the gross world, such

motives do not seem to be conspicuous in the literature, at any rate the non-dramatic literature, of the Renaissance. Whereas the romantic or modern outlaw is likely to be the special ideal of a cultural élite, or the helpless victim of a society that is condemned, I would suggest three propositions concerning the Renaissance hero: first, if he is "good," he is the magnified projection of an ideal generally accepted by society; second, if he is not "good," the pity and terror he evokes still leave the audience confirmed in their attachment to traditional values because these are also the values of the author, who is not—as critics so often say of modern writers —"seeking a new ethic"; and, third, whether he is good or not, and whatever divine or diabolical prompting he may receive, the Renaissance hero makes his own choices and is responsible for what he does. People more modern-minded than I might say that the first two propositions are tame and unexciting and that the third embodies an obsolete fallacy; I would say that all three help largely to explain the strength of Renaissance literature.

In point of time, the English Renaissance is far closer to us than it was to ancient Rome or the still more remote antiquity of Greece, but the Renaissance hero is far closer to Achilles and Agamemnon, Odysseus and Aeneas, Orestes and Oedipus, than he is to Leopold Bloom or Kafka's K or Frederic Henry or Isaac McCaslin or Willy Loman. This obvious fact is too large and vague to be in itself very enlightening, and we might recall some ways in which the classical ideal was assimilated and modified by Renaissance writers. To do so is to run over many commonplaces, but I for one have never been afraid of them, and, what is more important, writers of the Renaissance' were not.

In the first place, it is impossible to exaggerate the veneration authors and readers felt for the ancient thinkers, poets, historians, orators, statesmen, and generals as a race of superior beings. Such hero-worship was bred in the bone, and no amount of drill in grammar and rhetoric could kill it. Ancient *exempla* and *sententiae*, collected by Erasmus and others, embodied oracular wit and wisdom helpful for every contingency in life. Such anecdotes and aphorisms did not appeal merely to the Poloniuses of the world; they fertilized and sustained so emancipated a moralist as Montaigne, whose chief teachers were Seneca and Plutarch. The name of Plutarch is alone enough to recall this whole way of thought and feeling; and Sir Thomas North, in his racy and eloquent translation of the *Lives*, seems to view the ancient heroes both as remote demigods and as Elizabethans writ large. From Thomas Wilson's *Arte of Rhetorique* to Milton's *Of Education*, Renaissance humanists cherished the faith that boys who learned and recited the utterances of the Greeks and Romans could not but become like them. Thus the Renaissance author, brought up to worship and emulate the ancients, became thereby a conscious link in a great tradition, a member of the European community. Of course the universally held doctrine of imitation, itself an inheritance from antiquity, could and did engender a swarm of epics and dramas which, as Porson said of Southey's epics, will be read when Homer and Virgil are forgotten; but we are not concerned with that underworld of the dead.

Secondly, numerous ancients, from Aristophanes and Plato to Plutarch, had affirmed the didactic function of literature, and this principle was reaffirmed by a much fuller chorus of Renaissance poets and critics throughout Europe. What in our time has been labeled "the didactic heresy" was the basic theory of literature for some twenty-two centuries. Renaissance critics and poets have little to say about self-expression or the agonies of creation, but they are never weary of insisting that literature is philosophy teaching by examples, that it moves men to the love and practice of virtue and the abhorrence of vice. Thus the aim of literature is identical with the aim of education, virtuous action. We think of Sidney's frequent appeal, in his *Defense of Poesy*, to good and bad examples in classical epic and drama; of that epitome of Renaissance doctrine, Spenser's letter to Ralegh about *The Faerie Queene*, which presents a thoroughly didactic view of the famous heroic poems from Homer to Tasso; of Chapman's worship of Homer as the supreme poet and teacher, the creator of Achilles, the man of perturbation and physical courage, and Odysseus, the man of wisdom and unconquerable endurance. As recent interpreters of Chapman's humanism have shown, the principals in his tragedies tend to fall into two types, that of Achilles and that of his ideal hero, Odysseus.

This positive faith in the efficacy of both moral precepts and exemplary heroes must be emphasized because it is so far from anything we are accustomed to nowadays. If in modern novels we come on a character who appears to be "good," we are likely to assume that the author's intention is ironical; and we are left uncertain whether the other characters represent depravity or a new and elusively recognizable kind of virtue. Doubtless many persons would say that the difference is between naïveté and sophistication, but even they might hesitate to apply the word "naïve" to Shakespeare, who rarely leaves us uncertain about good and evil. And in general the great writing of the Renaissance is the product of educated, disciplined, realistic maturity; its idealism is not naïve or sentimental or spurious. Unlike a number of current writers of fiction, Renaissance authors had not discovered the fountain of perpetual adolescence.

Some other elements in this idealism may be briefly noted. Renaissance heroes, like classical heroes, are eminent in

94

worldly position as well as in character. High birth implies high advantages and imposes high obligations; moral success or failure is so much the more impressive and far-reaching in its effects. Willy Loman cannot declare, "Ay, every inch a king"; nor can the bedraggled heroine of *A Streetcar Named Desire* proudly say "I am Duchess of Malfi still," or

> Give me my robe; put on my crown. I have
> Immortal longings in me.

Pathetic derelicts have only the souls and the language of pathetic derelicts.

The Renaissance hero was not merely of lofty station; his moral stature, his personality, was commonly enlarged to something like superhuman dimensions. We never think of Shakespeare's tragic heroes as being mere men who could mix with the sober or the glamorous members of Elizabeth's or James's court and council. Of the factors that contributed to the creation of heroes beyond life size, one is negative and general: that imaginative writers were not in bondage to actuality, to dogmas about verisimilitude. Such dogmas did develop in the course of the seventeenth century and led into the Augustan age; but the narrative or dramatic poet of the earlier time was free to make his characters larger than life, to involve them with the supernatural, to do anything at all that he could bring off. Such freedom was a heritage from many things, including the heroic poems and romances of antiquity and the Middle Ages and the nonrealistic allegorical tradition. One positive and concrete symptom of Renaissance idealism is the classical mythology that writers used so much, often flatly, but often too with inspired potency. Mythological allusions could be a language of superhuman significance and intensity. The gods and goddesses and heroes represented power, passion, beauty, greatness in good or evil, beyond human limitations. Examples are everywhere from Spenser and Marlowe through Shakespeare to Milton.

Finally, not to prolong these generalities, we may remember that the English Renaissance was, historically, an ideal period for the imaginative writer. The planets, so to speak, were in such a conjunction as could never have occurred before and could never occur again. Writers of that age were not self-consciously agonizing over their alienation from society, over lost sources of power, over the extinction of "myth." They had, in abundance, their own problems, universal and particular, but everything they needed, as poets, was there. The texture of everyday life was at once brutally realistic and sublimely miraculous. Christian belief, in its full fundamentalist and anthropomorphic drama, was—except for a very few sceptics—an all-embracing and immediate reality. The great world and the heart of man were alike the battle ground between God and his angels and Satan and his agents of evil. Within the Christian frame, human life was closely interwoven with both the familiar processes and the mysteries of nature, from the influence of the stars and celestial portents of disaster down to such direct acts of God as frost and flood and the recurring plague. Man was not alone in a mechanized and meaningless universe; he was midway between the beasts and the angels, a being of immortal destiny in a divine order. This was, too, an age in which the English language was in its fresh, rich maturity, with none of its infinite capacities blunted and debased. And one might add that writers, even if they did not get beyond school, were commonly well educated.

For the heroic strain in literature, then, it was of prime significance that writers, most of the characters they created, and most of their readers or hearers looked up as a matter of course to persons and conceptions above the common level.

The Isolation of the Renaissance Hero

The persons they looked up to ranged from God and the angels down to the sovereign and the aristocracy; the conceptions from the Christian view of life and the world down through philosophic ideas to the ordinances of law and the conventions of society. These persons and conceptions, to be sure, were not of equal sanctity, yet in actual life and in literature (apart from comedy and satire), the mass of people, including writers, were respectfully or reverently aware of planes of being above their own. Nowadays, angry young men in England and beatniks in the United States might conceivably be revolted by this picture of "the Establishment," of a nation of "squares," but it has no small bearing on the nature of the hero in Renaissance literature.

Recalling again the cliché about the alienation of the artist, we might, at first thought, say that the Renaissance writer was in a partly similar position. In Europe generally, through much of our period, artists of all kinds might be dependent on royal or noble patronage; writers of noble or gentle birth might disdain the degradation of print; more or less learned writers, aristocratic or bourgeois, like Sidney or Chapman or Jonson or Milton, might scorn the profane multitude and might have a scholarly or a religious sense of dedication to the high office of seer and teacher. Thus, as I said, the Renaissance writer might seem to be, and to have a consciousness of being, set apart from and above his fellows.

Yet, in relation to our subject, these facts are much less important than the fact that serious, educated writers, who came mostly from a sober middle class, had, and knew they had, a sympathetic audience; they were not talking to themselves in a great void. The point is that the elements of Renaissance idealism that have been outlined were held in common by writers and readers—held, to be sure, on varying levels of sophistication, but held none the less. Even the so-called

97

aristocratic outlook, the respect for rank and authority, was shared by such middle-class poets as Spenser and Shakespeare and by their middle-class as well as their courtly audience; it was an integral part of the social and religious order and atmosphere. Shakespeare, cut off as a dramatist from direct commentary, can and does rely on the uniform moral sense of his socially heterogeneous public, Spenser does not have to persuade sceptical readers that traditional conceptions of holiness, temperance, and the other virtues are universally valid; his readers, whatever their individual lapses, believe that firmly already and are prepared to see those virtues and their opposites in action.

It is needless to recall the details of Spenser's fables. His heroes—and Britomart—are examples *par excellence* of the Christian-classical creed which was a general possession. These characters move through what is outwardly the world of romance but essentially the world of everyday experience, a world crowded with persons representing all shades of good and evil. Even Prince Arthur, who stands above other knights, participates in action in accordance with his inclusive virtue of magnificence or magnanimity, or as the agent of grace or providence. *The Faerie Queene*, in addition to being much else, is a conduct book in verse, and Spenser's outlook is thoroughly social and normal. The Red Cross Knight, sick at heart from former guilt, longs for contemplative seclusion, but, as a good Protestant, he knows that he must return to the life of action and trial. One small item may be cited because we happen to know how two young romantic poets reacted to it. In the second canto of the fifth book, after the destruction of a pair of upper-class extortioners, a giant who is beguiling the mob with specious demands for communistic equality is, after debate, pushed off the cliff by the arm of justice. Shelley and Keats were both admirers of Spenser but both, independently, resented this act as typical of the way in which power deals with those who question economic and social orthodoxy. Such an attitude might be expected from young liberals of the revolutionary age. But Spenser's attitude was that of all sober Elizabethan citizens, who knew the perils to which their small country was exposed from without and within and who prized stable order above all things. Shakespeare, whose contempt for the fickle mob is amply apparent, took the same view of Jack Cade's rebellion.

Of the many affinities between the sage and serious Spenser and Milton, the most obvious and central is their Christian faith, their Christian view of life and Christian scale of values, although Spenser reflects more broadly his own and his age's concern with Renaissance ethics and culture, while religion animates and dominates Milton's writing. And while Spenser, in his letter to Ralegh, celebrated the virtues of Agamemnon and Ulysses and the rest, Milton, who owed so much to the classical epics, expressly repudiated their materials and themes and took the bold step of investing his epic villain, God's adversary, with the heroic qualities of the traditional epic hero; he could rely on his early readers' recognizing the inadequacy and the complete corruption of such qualities. In doing so he did not anticipate romantic criticism of the nineteenth century or those modern critics of nineteenth-century vintage (in Miltonic matters) who apparently cannot understand a Christian and mythic poem.

Whereas Spenser's protagonists are immersed in the active world, Milton's are conspicuously isolated, Adam in the nature of the case, Christ and Samson by dramatic design. The Red Cross Knight and Adam are both Everyman (Eve is not Una but Everywoman), and Adam also has Guyon's right reason, although it is perverted. Unlike Red Cross and Guyon, Adam cannot mix with mankind, but, along with his higher endowments, he has his full share of human frailty. In the stories of both Red Cross and Adam there are two heroes, the man who falls into sin and the one greater man who enables the sinner to enter upon the way of salvation—although there is a difference between Prince Arthur and the Son of God. Further, both Red Cross and Adam, stricken by guilt, would welcome death, but the vision of both is cleared and both are given the strength to renew the life of duty in the world, which for Adam is no longer idyllic Eden but the grim world of history; it is through Michael's presentation that Adam is linked with all human experience and sin. And, to go no further with affinities, both Spenser (in *Mutability*) and Milton (repeatedly in the later books of *Paradise Lost*) themselves turn away from the troubled and sinful life of earth to a heaven of peace and order and innocence—poignant utterances all, and perhaps especially for Milton, who had striven so long for the establishment of Christ's kingdom among men.

If Christian faith and the Christian scheme have not been available to most modern writers, as they were not to the ancient pagans (although there may be partial parallels in both), we might say that pagan, Christian, and modern heroes stand on common ground by virtue of their acquiring a new and profound self-knowledge. Some kinds of self-knowledge, to be sure, do not go much beyond Parolles' "Simply the thing I am / Shall make me live"; but we are not concerned with these. In one of the greatest scenes in the *Iliad*, and in literature, the callous Achilles learns compassion; Odysseus is a wiser man from the start, yet he grows in wisdom. The *Aeneid* has a more recognizably religious frame and atmosphere, and in the fulfillment of his mission Aeneas gains understanding through trial and error and divine guidance. But the heroic knowledge that Red Cross and Adam learn is the Christian gospel of love and faith, humility and obedience, which alone can overcome evil. Christian self-knowledge and natural self-knowledge can merge, yet they are distinct. Even Satan has a tincture of the former, and it deepens his tragic potentialities, since, whatever his public harangues, he has a conscience that tells him, in soliloquies, what he was and is and might have been. Yet, in his imaginative realization of Satan, Milton did not allow those tragic potentialities to develop beyond a strict limit and then extinguished them altogether; if Satan were made a really tragic figure—something that Milton, being Milton, could never have done anyhow—the poem, as he conceived it, would collapse.

In Milton's two last works the isolation of the hero is set in high relief. It could be said, in terms that cover romantic and modern literature, that this is the isolation of a superior being in a corrupt world; but there are of course essential differences. In *Paradise Regained* Christ is presented in his human role, meeting the trials that Everyman meets, but with the invulnerable strength given by virtues that Adam could only hope to attain. Having light from above, Christ needs no other, not even the moral wisdom of Greece—although he possesses and uses it. We increasingly feel his isolation not only from the world of historical actuality and Satan's bribes but from the people about him; his simple-minded disciples expect him to establish an earthly kingdom and even his mother does not understand him. Satan, so often foiled, can exclaim, with a potent mixture of conscious and unconscious irony:

> Since neither wealth, nor honor, arms nor arts,
> Kingdom nor empire pleases thee, nor aught
> By me proposed in life contemplative,
> Or active, tended on by glory, or fame,
> What dost thou in this world?

Throughout, Christ shows the superhuman perfection of the

Renaissance hero, and in answer to the final challenge both he and Satan receive proof of his divinity.

Samson, the purely human sinner, outwardly isolated as a blind, helpless captive, inwardly as estranged from God, moves from lacerated pride, from preoccupation with his misery and shame, through humble contrition to renewed faith; but that bald statement describes a drama that is charged with irony from the title and the first line onward. Our sense of the hero's isolation steadily deepens because neither friends nor enemies understand what is going on in his soul, and even his father and the Chorus do not grasp the full meaning of his final victory. In his early revolutionary prose Milton had been inspired by boundless confidence in men and movements; in his three late poems he takes his stand on the impregnable ledge of rock that experience has left him, faith in God and the integrity or the regenerative strength of the humble individual soul.

One bridge between the heroic poem and the theatre would be Shakespeare's history plays, his epic dramatization of "the Tudor myth"—in which a king might become isolated by incompetence or evil-doing—but it is the tragedies that concern us, and only a few familiar questions can be asked about the situation of the tragic hero.

Such heroic poems as those of Spenser, Chapman, and Milton are openly and deeply rooted in the Christian humanism of the Renaissance. The world of Elizabethan and Jacobean tragedy is a world of passion, violence, crime, and horror which may appear wholly secular and naturalistic and which, because of dramatic objectivity, may leave us at times uncertain of its author's attitudes. Shakespeare has been viewed as everything from a great heathen and muddled sceptic to an allegorical expounder of the Atonement. But it seems to be agreed that he was in accord with the religious beliefs and general outlook of his fellow citizens, however far his imaginative insight carried him beyond that level; and probably this holds for most of the other serious dramatists. The only one who can be labeled doctrinaire, George Chapman, found dramatic correlatives for his Christian-Platonic-Stoic humanism, and we have observed how his protagonists partake of his Homeric dichotomy: Bussy, a man of "outward fortitude," is isolated by his passion and pride, Clermont by his inward Stoic wisdom.

Some of our earlier generalities about Renaissance writers apply to the dramatists as well as the heroic poets—tragic heroes are likewise of exalted station, and larger than life—but there are divergences and added complexities. The tragic hero, in Shakespeare most of all, is above the common level in imaginative sensibility and the gift of utterance, qualities which bulk large in the total effect. In the sphere of action, tragedy shows what men do, not what they ought to do. The epic hero, while not perfect, must be less imperfect than most tragic heroes; the epic role would hardly fit Tamburlaine or Macbeth or Coriolanus or Antony. The epic hero, whatever his failures, achieves some kind of triumph and remains alive; the tragic hero meets outward and sometimes inward ruin that is completed by death. Here we may remember some historical antecedents of Elizabethan tragedy. It inherited the conception of the fall from high estate, a conception kept gloomily alive by the multiplying tragedies of the very popular *Mirror for Magistrates*. The cause of the fall might be the turn of Fortune's wheel or, as in Shakespeare's first mature tragedy, *Julius Caesar*, a fatal flaw of character. (That brings up Aristotle and the systematic rigor with which some nineteenth-century criticism discerned a tragic flaw in all Shakespeare's heroes; but there may be such a vast disparity between the actual or alleged flaw and the catastrophe that the formula loses its meaning.) Then there was of course the degree to which Seneca and the Machiavellian tyrant shaped the revenge play and tragedy in general.

To quote my favorite Shakespearean critic, Geoffrey Bush, "The tragic vision concerns itself with different forms of evil: in Shakespeare's exploration of character divided from the world, his concern is with the evil of acting and believing without meaning." There is no formula that covers the kinds of isolation in which Shakespeare's tragic heroes find or place themselves, unless it is that, in diverse ways and degrees, if only in a momentary flash, they attain a truer knowledge of themselves and others. Hamlet is alone in his grief, in awareness of his father's murder, in his plans for action—alone, in short, against the evil of the world about him. But Macbeth is left more and more alone in evil, until the righteous world rallies its forces to end his career of outrage. Both Hamlet the avenging protagonist and Malcolm, who leads the avenging army against the protagonist, see themselves as instruments of heaven. On the other hand Othello, a simple, high-minded leader of men in a Christian world, is led into a hideous crime and, having thus lost his noble self, takes his life in a vain show of pagan magnanimity (although some readers would object to this last phrase). The pagan and passionate King Lear, having lost the trappings of royalty and everything but the love of Cordelia and Kent, learns before he dies the Christian virtues of humility, gentleness, and love. And the Roman Coriolanus and Antony are simply broken because they are the men they are.

A concluding word may be said about some contrasts that have been conventionally drawn between Greek and Shakespearean tragedy: that Greek turns on fate, Shakespearean on character; that Greek tragedy vindicates the moral order which an individual's acts and sufferings have appeared to shake or obscure, whereas the Shakespearean catharsis involves no such vindication but comes about through our feeling for a character whose greatness transcends defeat and death. These commonplaces contain as much error as truth. Fate, the incalculable play of event and circumstance, operates in both Greek and Shakespearean tragedy. If in Shakespeare no character is fated to commit the sins of Oedipus, what is it that causes "the fatal entrance of Duncan" into Macbeth's castle or brings Antony within the orbit of Cleopatra, that confronts Othello with a tale Hamlet would have promptly seen through and Hamlet with the need for an act that Othello would have promptly performed? The essential thing about Oedipus is not his unwitting sins of the past but his determination to find out the truth at whatever cost to himself; and Antigone, with clear knowledge of the consequences, chooses to obey divine rather than human law. As for the moral order, there is in Shakespeare no such religious and metaphysical solution as Aeschylus evidently had for the Promethean trilogy, although the establishment of the Areopagus in the *Oresteia* has a kind of equivalent in the succession of Fortinbras and the overthrow of Macbeth; and the assertion of a moral order in Sophocles is not quite so clear-cut as it is often assumed to be. In Shakespeare, throughout some tragedies runs an explicit or implicit assertion of a moral order in the world; through others, such as *King Lear,* at least an assertion of the traditional moral values of humanity. As A. S. P. Woodhouse has observed, whereas Macbeth defies the moral order, Hamlet —like Milton's Samson—perishes at last in giving effect to it: "They are on the side of the power—the overruling power— which destroys them." In general, we can say that the Greek dramatists and Shakespeare—and the heroic poets—are at one in assuming a moral order, or in showing either isolated human goodness unconquered by evil or the traditional moral sense of mankind rallying to oppose evil. Moreover, all these writers are linked together, and distinguished from many moderns, in that their heroes are not seen as helpless, unresisting victims of either fate or society; they make choices and are responsible for their acts, even though those acts and their consequences leave us facing the insoluble mysteries of life and character and circumstance.

A SELECTED BIBLIOGRAPHY

Adams, Robert P. *The Better Part of Valor: More, Erasmus, Colet, and Vives, on Humanism, War, and Peace, 1496–1535.* Seattle: University of Washington Press, 1962.

Allen, Don Cameron. *Doubt's Endless Sea: Skepticism and Faith in the Renaissance.* Baltimore: Johns Hopkins Press, 1964.

Baker, Herschel. *The Dignity of Man: Studies in the Persistence of an Idea.* Cambridge, Mass.: Harvard University Press, 1947. Reprinted as *The Image of Man,* Harper Torchbooks, 1961.

Baldwin, Thomas W. *William Shakspere's Small Latine & Lesse Greeke.* 2 vols. Urbana: University of Illinois Press, 1944.

Bolgar, R. R. *The Classical Heritage and Its Beneficiaries.* Cambridge: Cambridge University Press, 1954; Harper Torchbooks, 1964.

Bouwsma, William J. *The Interpretation of Renaissance Humanism.* Washington: Service Center for Teachers of History, 1959.

Bush, Douglas. *English Literature in the Earlier Seventeenth Century 1600–1660* (Oxford History of English Literature). Revised Edition. Oxford: Clarendon Press, 1962.

——————————. *Mythology and the Renaissance Tradition in English Poetry.* New Revised Edition. New York: W. W. Norton, 1963.

——————————. *The Renaissance and English Humanism.* Toronto: University of Toronto Press, 1939; latest edition, 1962.

Bush, Geoffrey. *Shakespeare and the Natural Condition.* Cambridge, Mass.: Harvard University Press, 1956.

Cassirer, E., P. O. Kristeller, and J. H. Randall, eds. *The Renaissance Philosophy of Man.* Chicago: University of Chicago Press, 1948.

Crombie, A. C. *Medieval and Early Modern Science.* 2 vols. New York: Doubleday (Anchor Books), 1959.

Curtius, Ernst R. *European Literature and the Latin Middle Ages.* New York: Pantheon Books, 1953; Harper Torchbooks, 1963.

Ferguson, Wallace K. *The Renaissance in Historical Thought: Five Centuries of Interpretation.* Boston: Houghton Mifflin, 1948.

Ferguson, Wallace K., and others. *The Renaissance: A Symposium*. New York: Metropolitan Museum, 1953; Harper Torchbooks, 1962.

Frye, Roland M. *Shakespeare and Christian Doctrine*. Princeton: Princeton University Press, 1963.

Fussner, F. Smith. *The Historical Revolution: English Historical Writing and Thought 1580–1640*. New York: Columbia University Press, 1962.

Gilmore, Myron P. *The World of Humanism 1453–1517*. New York: Harper, 1952; Harper Torchbooks, 1962.

Greene, Thomas. *The Descent from Heaven: A Study in Epic Continuity*. New Haven: Yale University Press, 1963.

Harbage, Alfred. *As They Liked It: An Essay on Shakespeare and Morality*. New York: Macmillan, 1947; Harper Torchbooks, 1961.

Hay, Denys. *The Italian Renaissance in its Historical Background*. Cambridge: Cambridge University Press, 1961.

Helton, Tinsley, ed. *The Renaissance: A Reconsideration of the Theories and Interpretations of the Age*. Madison: University of Wisconsin Press, 1961.

Highet, Gilbert. *The Classical Tradition: Greek and Roman Influences on Western Literature*. New York: Oxford University Press, 1949; Oxford Galaxy Books, 1957.

Hoopes, Robert. *Right Reason in the English Renaissance*. Cambridge, Mass.: Harvard University Press, 1962.

Hughes, Merritt Y. "The Christ of *Paradise Regained* and the Renaissance Heroic Tradition." *Studies in Philology*, 35 (1938), 254–77.

——————. "Spenser's Acrasia and the Circe of the Renaissance." *Journal of the History of Ideas*, 4 (1943), 381–99.

Johnson, Francis R. *Astronomical Thought in Renaissance England: A Study of the English Scientific Writings from 1500 to 1645*. Baltimore: Johns Hopkins Press, 1937.

Kendrick, Sir Thomas D. *British Antiquity*. London: Methuen, 1950.

Kocher, Paul H. *Science and Religion in Elizabethan England*. San Marino: Huntington Library, 1953.

Kristeller, Paul Oskar. *Renaissance Thought: The Classic, Scholastic, and Humanist Strains*. New York: Harper (Harper Torchbooks), 1961.

Kuhn, Thomas S. *The Copernican Revolution: Planetary Astronomy in the Development of Western Thought*. Cambridge,

A Selected Bibliography

Mass.: Harvard University Press, 1957. Reprinted, New York: Random House, 1959.

Lathrop, Henry B. *Translations from the Classics into English from Caxton to Chapman 1477–1620*. Madison: University of Wisconsin Press, 1933.

Lewis, C. S. *English Literature in the Sixteenth Century excluding Drama* (Oxford History of English Literature). Oxford: Clarendon Press, 1954.

Lord, George DeF. *Homeric Renaissance: The Odyssey of George Chapman*. New Haven: Yale University Press, 1956.

Lovejoy, Arthur O. *The Great Chain of Being: A Study of the History of an Idea*. Cambridge, Mass.: Harvard University Press, 1936; New York: Harper Torchbooks, 1960.

McNamee, Maurice B. *Honor and the Epic Hero: A Study of the Shifting Concept of Magnanimity in Philosophy and Epic Poetry*. New York: Holt, Rinehart & Winston, 1960.

Major, John M. *Sir Thomas Elyot and Renaissance Humanism*. Lincoln: University of Nebraska Press, 1964.

Martz, Louis L. *The Poetry of Meditation: A Study in English Literature of the Seventeenth Century*. New Haven: Yale University Press, 1954. Reprinted, Yale, 1962.

Nicolson, Marjorie H. *The Breaking of the Circle: Studies in the Effect of the "New Science" on Seventeenth-Century Poetry*. Evanston: Northwestern University Press, 1950. Revised Edition, New York: Columbia University Press, 1960.

Panofsky, Erwin. *Studies in Iconology*. New York: Oxford University Press, 1939; Harper Torchbooks, 1962.

Rees, Ennis. *The Tragedies of George Chapman: Renaissance Ethics in Action*. Cambridge, Mass.: Harvard University Press, 1954.

Sandys, Sir John E. *A History of Classical Scholarship*. 3 vols. Cambridge: Cambridge University Press, 1908–21.

Sarton, George. *Six Wings: Men of Science in the Renaissance*. Bloomington: Indiana University Press, 1957.

Seznec, Jean. *The Survival of the Pagan Gods*. New York: Pantheon Books, 1953; Harper Torchbooks, 1961.

Siegel, Paul N. *Shakespearean Tragedy and the Elizabethan Compromise*. New York: New York University Press, 1957.

Smith, Hallett. *Elizabethan Poetry: A Study in Conventions, Meaning, and Expression*. Cambridge, Mass.: Harvard University Press, 1952.

Spencer, Theodore. *Shakespeare and the Nature of Man*. New York: Macmillan, 1942.

Spingarn, Joel E. *Literary Criticism in the Renaissance.* New York: Columbia University Press, 1899; 2nd ed., 1908; reprinted, ed. B. Weinberg, New York: Harcourt, Brace & World, 1963.

Stein, Arnold. *Heroic Knowledge: An Interpretation of Paradise Regained and Samson Agonistes.* Minneapolis: University of Minnesota Press, 1957.

Svendsen, Kester. *Milton and Science.* Cambridge, Mass.: Harvard University Press, 1956.

Thompson, James W. *A History of Historical Writing.* 2 vols. New York: Macmillan, 1942.

Thorndike, Lynn. *A History of Magic and Experimental Science.* Vols. V–VI. The Sixteenth Century; Vols. VII–VIII. The Seventeenth Century. New York: Columbia University Press, 1941, 1958.

Tillyard, E. M. W. *The Elizabethan World Picture.* London: Chatto & Windus, 1943. Reprinted, Penguin Books, 1963.

Watson, Curtis B. *Shakespeare and the Renaissance Concept of Honor.* Princeton: Princeton University Press, 1960.

Weinberg, Bernard. *A History of Literary Criticism in the Italian Renaissance.* 2 vols. Chicago: University of Chicago Press, 1961.

Werkmeister, William H., ed. *Facets of the Renaissance.* Los Angeles: University of Southern California Press, 1959. Reprinted, New York: Harper Torchbooks, 1963.

Wilson, Harold S. *On the Design of Shakespearian Tragedy.* Toronto: University of Toronto Press, 1957.

Wind, Edgar. *Pagan Mysteries in the Renaissance.* New Haven: Yale University Press, 1958.

Woodhouse, A. S. P. "Nature and Grace in *The Faerie Queene.*" *ELH, A Journal of English Literary History,* 16 (1949), 194–228.

——————————. "Tragic Effect in *Samson Agonistes.*" *University of Toronto Quarterly,* 28 (1958–59), 205–22.

Woodward, William H. *Vittorino da Feltre and other Humanist Educators.* Cambridge: Cambridge University Press, 1897 (reprinted 1905).

——————————. *Studies in Education during the Age of the Renaissance 1400–1600.* Cambridge: Cambridge University Press, 1906 (reprinted 1924).